MW00578844

WHAT PEOPLE ARE SAYING ABOUT *A Second Day*

"To see life from both sides now" is a rare gift. To share that insight with others is a blessing. To create new language to engage in conversation on suicidal thinking transforms the lives of individuals and communities. This is the heart of A Second Day, a book that lifts the soul and quickens the heart.

The Very Reverend Rebecca L. McClain, Transition Consultant

Fe is a master at helping entire communities address the issue of suicide. Through his writing and speaking, he has a sensitive, engaging, and nonjudgmental way of equipping persons to talk openly and publicly without shame or worry.

Sandra Harstine, Former Managed Care Coordinator,
Mental Health and Recovery Services Board

A Second Day helped me reframe suicide. Instead of thinking of suicide as an act done by an individual isolated from everyone else, I have come to see suicide as a public health concern and as an act done, in large measure, as a response to community dynamics. Fe calls us as a community to address the dynamics that may lead people into the "night" of suicidal thinking.

David Miron, MSHRD, Instructional Facilitator in Comparative Religion

A Second Day provides us with a deeply personal perspective on suicide and a unique language to speak about this still taboo condition. The author brings hope to the hopeless while challenging us all to seriously think about how we might be a lifeline in our communities to those who suffer in isolation, rather than contributing to this isolation by creating toxic communities.

Rev. Dr. Scott Mitchell, PsyD, Clinical Psychologist,
President/CEO Samaritan Interfaith Counseling Center, Inc.

The current experience of many in their families, at work, and in their communities is marginalization through misunderstanding or just plain neglect. They don't fit in because no one bothered to know them. No one invited them to be who they are. Instead they were told to be only who others wanted them to be. Suicidal thinking can indeed be a response to this loneliness. A Second Day is a source of hope for these people and all of us.

Linda Karlovec, PhD, Therapist

In A Second Day, Fe Anam Avis articulates feelings that I had and have, and in doing so offered hope and support—I wasn't alone! He offers tools to help continue my second day journey. I go back to this book, especially when I am struggling, and it helps me to stay in the light of the second day and not slip back into the night.

Kelley Bowen

In A Second Day, Fe Anam Avis shares more than facts; he shares part of himself that allows survivors of the dark night of suicidal thinking to end their silence. At the same time he teaches us how to come alongside someone contemplating suicide and help him or her enter the second day.

Peg Earhart LISW, ACSW, Associate Professor Zane State University

Although this book is written about suicidal thinking, I found myself thinking about how it is a book for all of us who desire a change in our life—a death to the old and an embracing of a resurrected, transformed way of living and being.

Nancy Sayer, MS, LCPC, PCC, Director, Samaritan Center for Congregations

A SECOND DAY

A HOPEFUL JOURNEY OUT OF SUICIDAL THINKING

FE ANAM AVIS

A SECOND DAY
A Hopeful Journey Out of Suicidal Thinking

PUBLISHING CONSULTANT: Huff Publishing Associates, LLC
COVER IMAGES © Hikrcn | Dreamstime.com and © iulias | Dreamstime.com
COVER AND INTERIOR DESIGN: Marti Naughton

 PUBLISHED BY Magi Press
ISBN: 978-0-9787850-3-1

Scripture quotations marked as indicated are from:

CEV from the Contemporary English Version © 1995 American Bible Society.

ESV from the Holy Bible English Standard Version © 2001 by Crossway.

DBY from the Darby Bible Translation, first published in 1890 by Johnson Nelson Darby.

KJ21 from the 21st Century King James Version © 1994. Used by permission of Deuel Enterprises, Inc., Gary, SD 57237. All rights reserved.

THE HOLY BIBLE, NEW INTERNATIONAL VERSION®, NIV® Copyright © 1973, 1978, 1984, 2011 by Biblica, Inc.® Used by permission. All rights reserved worldwide.

Acknowledgements

The concept of acknowledgement takes on a whole new meaning for many Second Day persons who have found the strength to stay alive through the support of some very special persons I call "Othersouls."

My Othersouls include Jerry and Linda Karlovec, Harvey and Carolyn Weese, Don and Leta Cook, Vicki Rush, and Robyn Strain. These are the people who loved my Soul and refused to let go of me without a fight. My children spent one very difficult evening with me at a particular low point and, by their presence, gave me reason to live another day, and then another one, and yet another.

Much of this book grew out of the loving and wise counsel provided to me over a seven-year period of time by Dr. Azaria Akashi. Her constant attention to the wisdom of my Soul and her advocacy for my life was transformative.

I also want to acknowledge the many people in the suicide prevention community who have engaged me to facilitate and train in their communities. There are far too many to name. I am especially grateful to have worked with Six County Mental Health and Recovery Services as well as Appalachian Behavioral Health. Sandra Harstine has been a champion of suicide prevention efforts in her region of the state of Ohio and a tremendous professional ally. Melinda Moore had the courage to found the Ohio Coalition for Suicide Prevention and engaged me in the work of creating the Ohio Suicide Prevention Plan that guides Ohio communities to this day.

Don Cook served as my editor on this book and for that painstaking work and his many good suggestions has earned my undying gratitude. For this edition of *A Second Day*, I also want to thank Bill Huff, owner of Huff Publishing Associates for ably shepherding this book to completion, Susan Niemi for her sensitive and extremely helpful editing of the material, and Marti Naughton for the terrific cover design.

My wife, Shawn, is the embodiment of the biblical description of a love that never fails, always protects, always trusts, always hopes, and always perseveres. She came into my life during some of my darkest hours. Even when she was saying to herself, "I must be crazy. I am falling in love with a man who wants to kill himself," she stayed. We have watched the sunrise together, and I am blessed to share my Second Day with her.

I thank all the "Othersiders" in the world who have struggled valiantly through traumas large and small to land on a better shore. You give me courage.

Finally there is that Presence in the universe, persistent, insistent, and inescapably loving that is the source of every good gift and inspiration. I am guided. I am grateful.

Fe Anam Avis
Lent 2008

Contents

Preface

"We shall not cease from exploration
And the end of all our exploring
Will be to arrive where we started
And know the place for the first time."

I n these familiar words from "Little Gidding," poet T. S. Eliot
gives expression to the discovery that life has an odd sort of
luminosity. Having sharp modern minds trained to observe
cause and effect, we have no problem believing that our past
illumines our present, that the Child is the father of the Man
(William Wordsworth). Psychoanalytic theory proposes that
much of who we are today was shaped by the interactions of
our childhood.

What we are less prepared to accept is that our present casts
light on our past. We think we understand what is happening in
a particular moment of life as we live it. We believe that we could
give a full explanation of our activity should someone question
why we are doing what we are doing. Only later do we discover
that our explanation at that moment would have been seriously
deficient. The unfolding of future events discloses a purpose in our
past that was hidden in the moment. We are carried irresistibly
forward by the river of time into territory we could not have
guessed. Yet some of it seems strangely familiar. It is as if some

unseen intelligence had been preparing us prior to our arrival. Who has not looked back into his or her yesterdays to discover something had a purpose that could only be fully understood years down the stream of time?

When three young men in a small suburb of Columbus, Ohio, took their lives during a seven-month period of time spanning the end of 1997 and the beginning of 1998, my engagement in the tragedy seemed like a natural response from the pastor of the only church lying within the boundaries of that community. Together with my friend and colleague, Linda Karlovec, a PhD psychologist, we formed a coalition of parents, school officials, medical and mental health practitioners, business representatives, and clergy aimed at stemming the hemorrhage of lives from the youth of our community. This work ultimately became a model for other suicide prevention efforts across the state of Ohio and led me to acquire training in suicide awareness and intervention skills.

What I could not have known at the time was that suicide would become an active threat to my own life. Within three years, I was having spontaneous images of bullets going through my head. By the summer of 2003, I could not stop thinking about suicide. My life hit its nadir when I found myself standing at the counter of a sporting goods store to purchase a gun with which I intended to kill myself. In a desperate attempt to keep myself alive, I checked myself into a hospital emergency department.

This happened during a time when I was training thousands of people in suicide awareness and equipping many others with suicide intervention skills. Physician, heal thyself! Ironically, the skills I taught others were undoubtedly helping keep me alive. I thought I understood that my response to the three student suicides in my community was simply an appropriate act of leadership. I came to understand that the suicide prevention work was also preparing me for my own personal survival.

For a number of years I traipsed all over the region conducting awareness training using a curriculum entitled SuicideTALK. The objective of the training was to help people become comfortable enough with the topic of suicide to be able to ask others who appeared to be in trouble if they were thinking about suicide. "When you 'get' this training you will realize that anyone can be thinking about suicide," I would say. After the presentation had ended and the room cleared, one of the students who had hung back made her way over to me as I was packing up my overhead slides. "I have a question," she began. "Are you thinking about suicide?" Anyone, even a suicide prevention trainer, can be thinking about suicide. I think back on those days and realize there was a greater purpose at work than I knew at the moment. The very things I was teaching others would end up saving my own life.

As Joni Mitchell sang, "I've looked at life from both sides now," I have experienced life from the side of the suicide prevention trainer and from the side of the suicidal person. This book is a personal integration of those two sides. It is not intended to encompass every suicidal person's experience; it will fit some much better than others. The reasons that people contemplate suicide are complex and vary widely from person to person. Of one thing we can be sure: There are millions of people in our society who have seriously considered suicide and who are still alive among us! This book offers a new language for them and for those who want to support them and learn what they have to teach us.

Among older African American women, suicide is virtually nonexistent. Why?

It is fair to say I have a purpose that drives me in the work of suicide prevention. I feel that it is something compelling in my life, something I am destined to do, something wound tight into the core of my being. This is simply another way of saying it is an expression of my Soul.

A central theme threading through every chapter is that suicidal thinking is often a response of a benighted Soul, struggling to find authentic expression in communities that are hostile or indifferent to its existence. The Soul has a voice that will not be denied and a wisdom that is sound. Perhaps as we begin to give dignity to that wisdom we can begin to redirect the suicidal impulse to its more constructive purpose: transformation.

Most people attribute suicide to a variety of issues within the individual ranging from standard medical psychological diagnostic categories to selfishness to cowardice to sin. I am not a trained clinician. I leave the diagnostic research to experts in the field. I merely observe that in some communities, suicide is almost unheard of; in other communities, it is a leading cause of death. In our nation, for example, suicide is a leading killer of young people and older adult men. For older African American women, the rate is miniscule. When the suicide rate in one community (Native American youth) is seventy times the rate in another community (older African American women), it is reasonable to assume that there are factors in some communities that protect people from suicide and factors in other communities that inadvertently throw accelerant on the suicidal impulse.

There is one difficulty we must face head on. Suicide prevention work begins with the core assumption that many suicides can be prevented. This always runs the risk of leaving those who have lost loved ones to suicide with an increased burden of guilt. The truth is that all communities are a complex network of individuals and groups including not only families, but also schools, religious institutions, athletic teams, service organizations, businesses, clubs, social associations, and medical/mental health services all bound together by a culture of ideas and values that either protects individuals from suicide or contributes to their demise. It is a community problem that can only be addressed by a community response. It is unrealistic and unfair for this burden of creating a healthy environment to fall solely on families, no matter how highly we regard them.

We have made progress on a large number of medical and mental health fronts over recent years. Through large-scale public health efforts we have shifted the habits of Americans to wash their hands and cough into their sleeve to address the H1N1 epidemic. Through those and other efforts, only 12,000 persons died in that epidemic. We have made little progress in dealing with suicide that kills three times that many persons every year.

No community can consider itself robust and thriving if persons living in it do not want to live any more. How we can create communities where large numbers of people do not want to kill themselves is not a question for a few to answer, but an essential question of our time. Addressing the issue of suicide requires that we address many other critical issues along the way that will lead to stronger communities for all of us. Nothing less than a fundamental shift in how we understand the purpose of our lives on this planet and how we live together will do. In the meantime, we must save individuals one at a time and learn all that we can from people who have discovered a Second Day.

Fe Anam Avis
January 25, 2014

Introduction

During the past fifteen years, I have been granted the privilege of speaking to thousands of persons about a topic I would never have imagined in my early career: suicide. I generally close with this story.

I was sitting at my desk one day when a name flashed across the screen of my mind accompanied by the urging to call her on the phone. I began the conversation with the usual civilities and then dove right into it.

"Gwen, are you okay?"

"Yes, I am fine," she responded with a deserved wisp of puzzlement in her voice. "Why?"

"I don't know. I just felt that I should call you." There was an uncomfortable moment of awkward silence.

"Well, good," I said clumsily. "Can I, um, just pray for you on the phone?"

She consented and the call ended soon after. I hung up the phone with the usual neurotic berating of myself!

"That was a stupid thing to do!"

About a year later, I was sitting with a small group. During a time of sharing, Gwen, a member of the group, blurted out, "Of course, Russ* saved my life."

She caught my bewildered reaction (I had forgotten about the phone conversation months before) and followed with, "Someday, I will tell you the story."

---

*Russ is my former name and continues to be the business name I use in my consulting work with organizations.

1

We can keep our sanity and stay alive as long as there
is at least one person who is waiting for us.
A life-saving relationship can develop in an hour;
one eye movement or one handshake can replace years
of friendship when a person is in agony. *Henri Nouwen*

Gwen kept her promise. It seems that on the day I had called she had just received some devastating news. She had sent her husband away, pulled his handgun out of the gun closet, and loaded it. Just then, the phone rang.

"I was too ashamed to tell you the truth," she confessed. "But I took it as a sign that God wanted me to live. I put the gun away, walked outside to a chair on the patio, and gave my life to God."

I tell that story at the end of a day of training to make three simple points.

First, there are people in our lives that we know and love who are secretly considering suicide.

Second, regardless how clumsy we may feel, simple acts of care, offered on a hunch, are often amplified by some mysterious grace to become signs of divine love in a moment of utter despair and desperation.

Third, many persons like Gwen live among us. They have found a way out of the pattern of suicidal thinking. This book is named for these "Second Day" persons.

I know there are many Second Day persons because I always invite them to speak to me at the end of a presentation. Inevitably, in a group of just about any size, one or more persons make their way forward to say simply, "Hi. I am a Second Day person." There are often tears, hugs, and even laughter, but, unfailingly, a sense of relief. For most, I am the first person they have ever told. There is nothing special about me that triggers this disclosure except that I am one of them.

The journey out of suicidal thinking is not an even one. There are fits and starts. There is progress and relapse. Once that possibility of ending one's life has become a neighborhood familiar to the mind, it is easy to visit it again. As one Second Day friend said to me, "We must be vigilant."

This book is intended to be a friend on the other side of town, the life side. Like any friend, its fortifications are often required with some regularity or in particular moments of distress. There are few vaccinations for the mind that render our thinking invincible once and for all. We must nourish the life within us and repoint the brick at the foundation from time to time.

We tend to remember our mistakes and forget our lessons. Even after authoring this book, I find it important to pick it up every now and again to remind myself not only of the path of life, but also of the early signs that I am slipping off the bank— somewhere short of the rapids where it is easier to scramble back up to solid ground.

Persons who have never considered suicide also need gentle reminders of the secret vulnerabilities of those about them. Suicide, like many other human conditions, catches people on that fine line between tragedy and redemption. Where so much is at risk to be lost, much also stands to be gained. As *The New York Times* columnist David Brooks put it in his Op-Ed "The Irony of Despair" on December 5, 2013, "A person enters the situation amid feelings of powerlessness and despair, but once in the situation the potential suicide has the power to make a series of big points before the world. By deciding to live, a person in a suicidal situation can prove that life isn't just about racking up pleasure points; it is a vale of soul-making, and suffering can be turned into wisdom."

Redemption is powerful in all its expressions. This book invites us to add the voices of Second Day persons to the chorus of others who in the face of overwhelming difficulties have found life snatched from the jaws of despair.

A Second Day

I am the faint light of the street lamp
 poking through your bedroom blinds
 to fall across your face
 when the drowsiness of death
 pulled down on your eyelids.

I am the surprise party you almost missed
 the one when you caught her
 looking at you in wonder,

  The phone call you took on the last ring
  from someone just thinking of you.

I am the heart you almost shattered
 and the laughter you almost silenced,
 a hundred close calls in a row.

I am the thin beams of a sunrise,
 slivers of hope dueling with darkness.

I am the life that has always called your name
 and the one you have always longed for,
 the friend who keeps getting you into trouble,
 but will never leave you.

I am the morning you almost gave up on
 and the light that could never give up on you.
I am your Second Day.

Fe Anam Avis

— ONE —

The Missing Note

n the next hour, four persons in the United States will kill
themselves.[1] One of them will leave a note explaining why
he or she found life too painful to continue living. In that same
hour, millions more will think about killing themselves . . . and
decide not to. Almost none of the latter will send someone a note
explaining why he or she decided to live. This fact alone reveals the
curious nature of our attitude toward suicide—the subject is so
frightening that the person who dies by suicide does not feel safe
talking about it until he or she is dead. By that time, conversation
is no longer a possibility. As a result we end up knowing more
about what makes for death than what makes for life.

   If this were the case with any other fatal condition, say cancer,
we would find it quite peculiar. Imagine that thousands of people
were surviving a particularly deadly type of cancer but we never
took the time to discover why they were surviving. Yet, we have in
our midst millions of people who have personally survived their
own suicidal thinking, and we almost never ask them what kept
them alive. We often have the suicide note. The "this is what kept
me alive" note is missing. Society cannot help but be on the wrong

---

1   In this book I will not be using the phrase "commit suicide" since "commit" implies
     a crime. Suicide is a tragic, but not criminal act.

road when our maladies are public but our cures (how to stay alive) are kept private and unexplored. In the suicide prevention communities that have embraced me, I have not found an adequate language for those like me who have emerged from the grip of suicidal thinking. The word *survivor* immediately comes to mind as an option. However "survivor" is almost exclusively used to refer to those who have had someone in their family or a close friend die by suicide. Using this definition, there are approximately 4.6 million survivors of suicide in the United States who have either lost a family member or close friend to suicide.

The key to life is to turn pain into insight.
Insight is not an answer to why things happen.
It is an awakening to what is real.

However, there are at least twenty million people in the United States who have seriously considered suicide but have not killed themselves. That's why I have coined the term Second Day persons. Second Day persons are those who have found deliverance from the grip of suicidal thinking.

I am a Second Day person. My life can be divided into three time periods, a First Day, a Night, and a Second Day. (I am using the word *day* to mean an indeterminate period of time that could cover hours, months, or years.) The First Day was that span of time I lived without considering suicide as an option. The Night consisted of that period when suicide was not only a real option but impossible to erase from my thinking. The Second Day is the season in which I now live, a season in which I have made the necessary changes to find life worth living.

It sounds strange to demarcate life in such a way, such as my children who used to measure clock time by a television program (number of "Brady Bunches") and calendar time by the number of "sleeps." Children innately measure time by experiences. We have to be taught how to tell time using a clock. To speak of a First Day, a Night, and a Second Day that are measured out, not by a calendar, but by the experience that characterizes those seasons is to return to a deep, primal pattern that I find healing. If we are to repair the neural patterns that are rooted in our primal past, we must return to the thinking of our childhood and grow up anew. I am a Second Day person who is quite a number of "sleeps" old. I have to pick up my wife in about four "Brady Bunches."

There are many more Second Day persons living among us than we may realize. They worship beside us in our churches, synagogues, and mosques. They work beside us at our jobs and sit beside us in our classrooms. It would surprise us to discover them within our circle of friends or even within our own families. But they are surely there.

I was having tea several days ago with a friend I had not spoken to for some time. When we finally settled ourselves at a table, I shared with her that I was working on this book and that I was a Second Day person. She looked at me with a sense of relief.

"I, too, am a Second Day person," she disclosed. "In fact, I am giving a speech about my experience in two weeks."

Oddly enough, what we can learn from Second Day persons is not so much what makes people want to kill themselves, but a perspective on the joy of living. I just received a card from my friend. Above her name she had written, "Every day is a bonus." This is only one of the important lessons about living we can learn from those who almost decided not to.

Second Day people have much in common with family members who are survivors. Both groups are dealing with the devastation that suicide visits upon individuals, families, friends, and communities. But they are looking at suicide from a different vantage point. Second Day people are celebrating their liberation and are seeking to sustain a resurgent zest for living. Second Day people may grieve the losses of the Night—relationships, career, or social status—but many have come to understand that such losses were necessary to their own growth and, hopefully, the growth of others.

If you follow the thread of your deepest longing, it will lead to the inn of your happiness . . . but you may have to sleep in the rain on the way.

Even in many suicide prevention communities, Second Day persons are black-holed. The shame that they would seriously consider suicide and the fear of others' negative reactions is so strong that the light of their learning cannot escape into their communities. Many suicide prevention meetings are conducted without acknowledging the presence of persons in their meetings who may be considering suicide or who may have survived the Night of suicidal thinking. As a result, we may hear many stories about lives coming to a tragic end, but far fewer stories of how lives were reclaimed by love and hope.

A primary factor in suicidal behavior is a sense of isolation. Ironically, Second Day people continue to find themselves extremely isolated. They suffer all the stigmatizing responses experienced by those who are actively suicidal. They fear that their self-disclosure will compromise their careers, their relationships, and their standing in the community. In addition, members of the suicide survivor community may be so focused on coping with their own devastation that it may be difficult for them to deal with a person who is seriously considering suicide or who is celebrating his or her own escape from the Night.

Second Day persons need the embrace of the suicide prevention community as an important step toward ending their isolation. This embrace can begin with simply acknowledging the presence of Second Day persons. By reducing isolation, this acknowledgement adds another protective factor to the Second

Day person's arsenal. It also offers hope to those struggling to find the courage to disclose their own suicidal thinking. It makes the lessons learned in the Night and in the Second Day available to the suicide prevention community.

Love with all your heart. A bird cannot half fly.

I want to be known as a Second Day person in the suicide prevention community. I want to meet and celebrate with other Second Day persons. I also want to reach back to those in the Night and help them find a way forward. I want to equip First Day persons with enough understanding of the Night so that they can feel better prepared to touch those who are struggling with suicidal thinking.

Carl Jung believed that addiction is a manifestation of a profound spiritual yearning, a thirst for wholeness that is part of the fundamental dilemma of being human. I believe that the suicidal impulse can also be the expression of a deep, spiritual wisdom of the Soul, valid, but wrongly interpreted. Once you have decided to honor this wisdom and yet live, the path forward must be transformational. It may also be extremely difficult. If you decide that your life is more important than death, it becomes more important than most everything else—including the expectations of those closest to you.

It is for this reason that a Second Day is not merely a repeat of the First Day. A Second Day person is not simply a First Day person who has stopped thinking about suicide any more than a caterpillar is a butterfly with its wings pulled off. A Second Day person may have experienced a transformation that often reaches to the heart of his or her existence. This is often a profoundly spiritual though not necessarily religious experience. In general, religious organizations are singularly First Day institutions. Their historic treatment of suicide using concepts of sin and hell, combined with their tendency to unintentionally fuel the suicidal impulse by ostracizing those who disappoint them, rule out many churches as spiritual communities where Second Day persons can step forward. Fortunately, many religious leaders are now catching a vision for how their communities can not only minister to those bereft by the suicide of a family member but also for engaging those considering suicide before it occurs.

Second Day people are part of a larger spiritual community of folks that I would call Othersiders. Othersiders are persons who have passed through a traumatic life experience that has required transformation as a condition of survival. Like suicide, alcohol and drug addiction are generally terminal conditions without some transformational intervention. Persons in the recovery community from such addictions are generally Othersiders. Othersiders usually believe that they have been delivered from their self-destructive impulse by a spiritual power. As Rabbi Dr. Abraham J. Twerski put it, and as often quoted by AA members, "Religion is for people afraid of going to hell. Spirituality is for those who have been there." This somewhat unorthodox perspective on life is one reason that Othersider communities are generally anonymous in nature.

People who are considering suicide are often viewed as having lost their faith. Ironically, people in the Night of suicidal thinking are often in a heightened state of spiritual awareness. While they are thinking about suicide, the fact that they are still alive indicates that they are actually ambivalent. A part of them wants to die, but another part wants to live. For many this ambivalence leads them to look for a sign that will guide them in their decision-making. As a result many Second Day people can tell stories of divine rescue resulting from powerful spiritual experiences.

What Second Day persons have discovered, along with their Othersider sisters and brothers, is that suicide invites us to explore the most fundamental aspects of our human journey—friendship and hope. These are as essential to the Soul as food and air are to the body. If friendship and hope could be wrapped into a capsule

The Missing Note 11

and administered by our communities, we would consider it a miracle drug.

The reality is that our society systematically and, in some cases, intentionally deprives people of both friendship and hope, and the happiness that is their by-product. Happiness on a large scale is an economic problem. It is not in our economic interests that people become generally happy. The goal of marketing is to bring people to the realization that they are unhappy so that they will subsequently buy something. The psychic toll that this is exacting upon us must be staggering. I say this provisionally because I do not know of any research to support it. But who would ever fund research that might demonstrate that our way of life is making us soul-sick? Not the corporations who depend upon our buying and consuming in ever increasing quantities. What happens if we discover to be true what research is already suggesting—the greatest risk factors for heart disease are not being happy in your life and not loving your work.

We are soul-sick for want of friendship and hope. Ironically, these are low-tech and generally within our reach. The issue of suicide poses to us the hopeful question of the Old Testament: "Why do you spend your money for that which is not bread. . .?" (Isaiah 55:2 ESV). It is a hopeful question because it assumes abundance, but abundance misspent. We can create communities that do a much better job of protecting one another from the ravages of isolation and despair.

This book is hopeful for you as a First Day person because it can help you understand how you can join the conspiracy of the universe to help save the lives of those in the Night. Take a moment and tally up the number of persons in your life who are important to you: family, friends, neighbors, work associates, members of spiritual communities and service organizations, sports teams you coach, and so forth. Now divide that total number by sixteen. On average, that's how many people in your life are thinking about suicide today. You don't have to be a surgeon, firefighter, or emergency medic to save a life. You can save a life by loving enough to listen with a smart, compassionate ear.

Even in the rare possibility that you will not personally be confronted by the issue of suicide, you may discover a zest for living from the lessons others have learned in the heart of darkness. Many people are living with a chronic sadness that may never lead to thoughts of suicide, but nonetheless dims the luminance of their Souls. I have never been addicted to alcohol, but my life has been enriched by the stories of those who have been. As a reader, you may never have seriously considered suicide, but you may find your own path brightened by those Second Day persons who have.

This book is hopeful for you as a person in the Night because it can help you realize that you are not alone, and that there is something right and true about your soul. And the Night is not forever.

This book is hopeful for you as a Second Day person because it joins hands with you in celebration, encourages you to continue in the pathways that sustain and protect your life, and calls forth a courage that reaches backward to those in the Night of suicidal thinking.

I had originally hoped to write this book with only occasional references to Christian scriptures. Alas, I found that I was unable. Because the issue of suicide is profound and touches on the deepest questions of our existence, it is an inescapably spiritual matter. I assure the reader that my frequent references to Christian scripture are not a surreptitious attempt to manipulate or exploit persons who are in a time of vulnerability with a religious agenda. I respect and honor every spiritual path. However, I cannot help but encourage those who are dealing with suicide to engage the spiritual roots of the issue. My hope would be that as you discover your own Soul on this issue new light will fall across the pages of your own religious tradition.

We have not all shared the experiences of this book, but we all have had a First Day. It is this First Day that is the subject of the next chapter.

TWO

The First Day

When you are living a life that is dominated by thoughts of suicide over a long period of time, it is sometimes difficult to remember what it is like to think otherwise. I suppose it is like growing older and discovering that you need reading glasses. After a while you become so accustomed to the blur that it is hard to remember exactly what it was like to see clearly from the end of your nose to the stars. You just know there was a "once upon a time" that was different.

Nevertheless, most of us who have seriously considered suicide as an option can remember that there was a time when we did not. I call it the First Day. The First Day begins with our birth and continues until the moment we seriously consider suicide as a solution to our problems. The First Day can be long or relatively short. For about twenty percent of us, our First Day ended at some point in high school. For others of us our First Day ended when we were young adults. Some of us have long First Days; we won't start thinking about suicide until we are in our 70s or 80s.

When you are in your First Day, the concept of suicide seems alien. You hear about this person or that one who suicides, and you wonder how someone could do such a thing. When I was ten years old, a boy who lived down the street came home from school one afternoon and killed himself. He was found hanging in the garage. In the days that followed, a friend and I would stand across the street with school books under our arms and stare at that garage.

People worry about the occasional lie told by choice. It is the necessary lies that destroy us. The measure of a society is the number of lies it requires just to survive.

"That's where he did it," we whispered. "Hanged himself. Why would he do something like that?"

Later we would take turns peeking into the garage through a crack in the green, plank doors while the other held our books and stood watch. We also took turns guessing about how it had happened and why.

As a First Day person you may find suicide to be an incomprehensible puzzle. You guess at it. You talk with other First Day people and you say things like: "I think that if someone wants to commit suicide, there's nothing you can do. They are going to do it. Right? Don't you think that's right?"

You hope you're right. As a First Day person, you may not know that suicidal thinking is similar to many other life-threatening conditions, and that early intervention can save a life. What do the following conditions have in common: diabetes, AIDS, heart disease, many types of cancer, and suicidal thinking? Answer: In each case early intervention can save lives. Can we save everyone? No. Will we sometimes fail others because we do not intervene quickly enough? Yes. Do we always urge people we love to get mammograms, prostate screenings, colonoscopies, blood pressure screenings, and cholesterol tests? Probably not. Do we always urge people we love to tell us if they are thinking about suicide? Probably not.

As a First Day person you probably don't think about suicide this way. Since you have never seriously considered suicide you can only project your optimistic state into the minds of others. It is difficult for you to grasp the number of people near you who are in the Night of suicidal thinking. It is a black fire that is burning down their future. It emits no light; it is as silent as the night. Again, put yourself in any room of sixteen persons. Family. Friends. Church. Work. Classroom. Clergy. On average, one of them is considering suicide. Understandably, as a First Day person you have trouble believing this is true.

We were all brought up in a First Day culture that has formed many of our attitudes regarding suicide. First Day culture has given us the impression that suicide is rare. In fact, it is the third-leading killer of high school students and the second-leading killer of young adults. When we look at the suicide rate (number of suicides per 100,000 persons) adult men over the age of eighty are killing themselves at five times the rate of teenagers. For every person that successfully completes suicide, it is estimated that as many as 100 self injure in a suicide attempt.

> ## The greatest problem for someone who is wrestling with suicide is finding someone to talk to.

Here is the wonderful truth in all this. Even if you are a First Day person who has never wrestled with the thought of suicide and cannot identify at all with a person who has, you can still help save a life. In spite of what society has taught you, the greatest problem for someone who is wrestling with suicide is simply finding someone to talk to. You can be a lifeline for someone struggling with suicide merely by listening to him or her.

The many stories I could tell to illustrate this point would exhaust you as a reader. Let me share two.

Several years ago *The New York Times* published a map of the United States with shading that was proportional to the suicide rate in the region. On that map was a dark circle over southeast Ohio. There are several possible reasons for this. High unemployment rates (hopelessness), shame about any form of weakness (isolation), and a hunting culture (available means). It is a beautiful part of the state with warm, hospitable people.

During the past several years I have conducted awareness training for thousands of people in that part of the state. My routine was generally the same. I would arrive early enough that I could stop at a local McDonald's for breakfast before going to the training site. One morning I was standing at a McDonald's counter looking at the menu panel. (I'm not sure why I was studying it for so long; it is not a complex menu!) I had my suicide awareness notebook on the counter in front of me.

I gradually became aware that there was a woman standing beside me who kept looking down at my notebook and then away as if she could not stand to keep looking at it. Finally, the tension broke. She tapped her finger on the cover of my notebook and said, "We need to do more about that!"

There is something beautiful just below the surface of the universe.
Sometimes when the wind blows from the east,
and the waters splash away, I catch a glimpse of it,
like a reef glimpsed from the corner of the eye,
just before a wave conceals it once again.
When I look for it directly,
it disappears like a god who forbids the mortal view.
But when I am content with a glance,
I am always aware of something astounding, just to the right.

"You're right," I nodded. "But why do you say that?"

There was a painful collecting of her thoughts. Then she blurted it out.

"Because my thirteen-year-old daughter hung herself two years ago and I can't get anyone to talk to me about it."

We sat down and had our breakfast together as she poured out the pain of losing her child. There was sadness and loneliness, tears and sorrow.

"Thanks for listening to me," she said as we left. "People usually cross the street to avoid me."

First Day people often believe that they will only create more pain by bringing up the subject of suicide; they usually don't realize how helpful they can be by simply listening with compassion and love. You don't have to be able "to relate"; you don't have to understand. In fact, it is best not to say that you understand. A non-judgmental, unconditional love can work miracles.

My second story occurred on a college campus. I was talking with a group of athletes. Interestingly enough, this group of incredibly strong and muscled students (any one of whom could have run me into the ground) was the most defensive group I have ever encountered. There were numerous side-bar conversations going on and laughter at the overhead slides I was projecting on the screen.

It all came to a halt when one of the men told his high school experience.

"My best friend killed himself. We were on the track team together. After he died, I started thinking about killing myself."

You could have heard the proverbial pin drop.

"I tried to tell people, but no one would listen. That was six years ago. For six years no one would listen to me. Until tonight."

For all its vastness, the universe is still smaller than the love that made you from it.

Our First Day culture unintentionally isolates people who are thinking about suicide by discouraging them when they try to talk. We may think that we are helping prevent suicide by refusing to talk about it. In reality, the "cure" of silence only makes the problem worse. It is like the nineteenth-century practice of bleeding patients who were suffering from various ailments. The intention to cure them was noble. However, not only was the treatment ineffective, it often hastened their deaths. When we discourage people from acknowledging their real experiences of life, we contribute to the fragmentation of their thinking and their isolation from community. If you are a First Day person you probably do not realize the power of your own loving presence.

But there is something else you probably do not realize: for many, your First Day will come to an end.

— THREE —

Evening

As many as eight out of ten persons will seriously consider suicide at some point in their lifetime. For many of us, our First Day will come to an end. This means that suicidal thinking is a common, though largely unshared experience of being human. It signals that something in our Soul needs attention. It also may be letting us know that a season in our lives is coming to an end.

**Long before Peter denied Jesus,
Peter denied Peter.**

My First Day ended when I was thirty-four-years old; I have vivid memories of that time. I had just moved my family from a rural, farming community to the city where I had grown up. I had been a pastor for about seven years. It is surprising for many to learn that research shows clergy to be more stressed and depressed than the general population. In addition, no particular set of beliefs about God is more protective against suicide than any other. Ironically, what many people spend so much time debating (conservative versus liberal, literal versus figurative, church versus synagogue) has little effect on keeping someone from killing him or herself. One of the gifts that research offers religious communities is to put our doctrinal disputes into proper perspective. It is the quality of the community life that appears decisive, not the particular belief about God.

Since we do not generally talk about such things in the church, I was unaware of the risks of suicide. What I knew was that we were moving to a new community. The new church I was called to serve as pastor was five times the size of my previous church, and I had little large church experience. I had never served on a church staff let alone led a church staff. But that was not what was bothering me.

In my first few days at the new church, I had read the minutes of the board meetings. I discovered that in the most recent meeting, the board had been divided over a major issue related to my call. In my first few weeks, I also discovered that I was at odds with a significant group of people in the church, namely the entire education committee. I had been successful in turning around my previous church. But here the real possibility existed that I could fail right here in my hometown. For reasons that would become clear to me later, the prospect of failure was insurmountably painful. How would I support my family? What would my parents think? How could I get another job? That's when it happened. For the first time in my life I said, "I could kill myself." Just like that, suicide had become an option to solve my problem. My First Day was coming to an end.

When suicide becomes an option on your list of possible solutions to a problem, you know you have entered Evening, the period leading to Night. You may argue in your own mind that this is not a serious problem since you have no intention of carrying it out. However, the fact that suicide has entered your thinking as a real solution is a signal that should not be ignored.

In retrospect, I wonder why I did not jolt myself into reality by asking this question: "If I had a problem with a person who was close to me and one of the solutions that I was considering was killing that person, could I live with that thought?" The obvious answer to the question is "No." "Why then, am I comfortable with the thought of killing myself?"

In my desperation I shared my thoughts with a friend who said he fully understood my feelings. This was helpful in that I didn't feel so alone. What I didn't come to grips with in that conversation was that my thoughts of suicide were a signal that something was seriously wrong. Unconsciously, I had just disabled the "ABOUT TO CRASH" warning light in my Soul. Suicide was a thought I could live with.

He practiced the end.

Being gone.

Strange. It was how he kept feeling.

You can love at the end.

No one can hurt you.

At the end, you love, you give,

you go to sleep.

The screaming doesn't touch you,

or the silence.

He practiced this.

He could keep feeling

by promising himself

he wouldn't be feeling tomorrow,

and there would be no pain.

But tomorrow came

and there was no love.

In the Evening you begin to get comfortable with the thought of suicide. Yes, comfortable is the right word. You think you have it under control, like a fire in a fireplace. In a strange way, it keeps you warm when the coldness of life's pain threatens to become more than you can handle. You get close to it in difficult times. Suicidal thinking helps you feel like you are not trapped all the while it is trapping you.

The problem is that you begin burning your future to keep the fire going. Long-term thinking begins to recede. You stop working to solve long-term problems in your vocation, in your relationships, and in your own self-development. You start taking risks for the thrill of it. During this time, I did my first sky dive and ended up with a badly broken ankle that required two surgeries to fix. I make no judgment on skydiving as a sport. I loved the experience. But in retrospect I probably could not have done it if I had not thought death a preferable option.

Then there is the second problem. The fire of suicidal thinking doesn't stay in the fireplace. Sooner or later it "jumps the hearth." You lose control. Short-term thinking begins to create more and more pain that fuels more suicidal thinking that leads to more short term thinking that leads to more pain. Eventually you come to the point where you can't stop thinking about suicide. Darkness has fallen.

You are in the Night.

FOUR

The Night

The Night is a black fire. If it were a red fire with crackling flames that mix with smoke to create a kind of yellow daylight, all would come running. I witnessed a house fire once. It was a cold winter night in western New York. A call had come in from the church phone tree. The Henderson house was burning. As I opened the door of my car, I glanced in the direction of the Henderson house some three miles away and could see that characteristic glow, so comforting in a fireplace, but so agonizing in the fifty-foot radius that defines a home. As it turned out, the wood the family had cut for the winter was too green and the resultant creosote had caught fire in the metal chimney pipe.

> Your angel will not catch you if you
> jump from a tall building tonight.
> But if you choose to have a Soul,
> your angel will carry you into a Second
> Day. Angels don't catch. They carry.

The starry night sky provided an incongruous backdrop to the scene of a family standing wrapped in blankets and watching their home burn down. Friends and neighbors were there. Men alternated between looking at the blaze and kicking the gravel around their feet. The women stood with arms folded and one hand covering their mouth as if to muffle a moan. The family talked about everything that was burning up at the instant of their speaking. It was like watching a creature die one limb at a time. They talked about the beginning of the house, how they had built it with their own hands, room by room. The funeral for their home had already begun and this one, like all funerals, began with a birth date.

The black flames of suicidal thinking are equally destructive but instead of burning down your past, they burn down your future. You start living as if you have no future. You don't maintain your car. You stop going to the dentist. You skip annual physicals. I remember turning fifty and watching Katie Couric demonstrate a colonoscopy on the *Today* show. Fifty is the magic year for getting your first one. I wondered what it was like to have a future I wanted to protect.

You stop planning for anything that is in the future. Payments into retirement plans and savings accounts make no sense. I would get notices from the Social Security administration about my retirement benefits and throw them away unread. Same with my pension fund. Eventually I stopped paying my city taxes.

Like a physical fire, a black fire burns down your future one room at a time. In fact it is killing your Soul piece by piece. Sooner or later, it begins to destroy your relationships. Your relationships, in a sense, are already over. You don't necessarily think about preparing people for your permanent absence because you don't perceive that they will lose anything of future value. People say that those who think about suicide are self-centered. In fact, many times the black fire makes us non-centered. The center has been burned down. It is gone. We assume that everyone feels about us the same way that we feel about ourselves. It is a kind of zero.

It is impossible to make a commitment because a commitment requires a future. You find yourself in relationship with people you love but you don't know what to say when they ask about a commitment. People assume you are afraid of commitment. The truth is that you are multiplying everything in the future by zero. How do you talk about a future nothing?

You hurt people who are in relationship with you because they have a future, and they assume a future with you. But when the black fire wipes out your future, it also threatens to wipe out the part of them that is connected to you. Sparks from your black fire jump to other lives. In a few cases the people closest to you begin to think of killing themselves, too. In other cases the black fire only destroys their future life with you. You can't imagine that to be much of a loss for them.

Like many physical fires, the black fire of suicidal thinking cannot be stopped at will. People say to you, "Stop thinking this way!" You can't. It is too powerful. It is like telling a fireman to instantly extinguish a brush fire that is burning out of control. I had spontaneous images of bullets going through my head. I couldn't stop them.

This doesn't mean that you can't accomplish anything in the Night. There is a kind of liberation that comes from assuming you have no future. You can take risks because there is little to lose. You find energy, not in the well of your own Soul, but by feeding on the hope of those who are close to you. During my Night, I wrote a book, my first book to be published. But I had to borrow the hope of my co-author in order to do it.

In the Night, you are generally ambivalent about suicide—there is a part of you that wants to die and a part of you that wants to live. You wander through bookstores looking for books that will provide practical guidance on how to kill yourself, but you do so cautiously for fear that someone will spot you. You decide you will kill yourself tomorrow, but when tomorrow comes you postpone it another day. Then you accuse yourself of being a chicken. You can't decide what is more cowardly, killing yourself or not killing yourself. Because all your mental processing is happening in isolation, you don't realize the kinds of distortions that are taking place. If you had someone in your life who could stand to listen to you without freaking, you might be able to talk yourself out of it. But you can't seem to find someone who wants to know.

I have eaten at the table of deception,
and drank the wine of lies.
It was a heady buzz with a long night of puking.
Truth makes a poor bride but is a tireless lover.

No one causes the black fire in the Soul of another. There are accelerants that make the fire burn faster and hotter. When I was a boy, we had a coal furnace in the house. My father would sometimes throw kerosene on the coal to get the fire going. I loved watching the fire come to life. Once I decided to sneak down to the furnace by myself and throw kerosene into it. I poured the kerosene into a coffee can and carefully replaced the cap on the spout. Unfortunately, I used much more kerosene than my father ever had because I wanted to create a larger flame. I opened the door of the furnace and threw the accelerant into a bed of coal in full blaze. The inevitable explosion of flames did no harm to me, but it left my hands quivering and my five-year-old legs trembling as I ran back up the steps.

The black fire is accelerated by isolation and loss of hope. When people reject or avoid someone who is in the Night of suicidal thinking, the power of that thinking is strengthened. It is like throwing kerosene. Other people do not start the black fire of suicidal thinking. No one can put suicidal thoughts into the mind of someone else by simply talking about it. But when you are in the Night, the black fire is accelerated by people who withdraw from you. You find that this thought never crosses the minds of people who exclude others because they assume that suicidal thinking is rare and only occurs in very sick or weak people.

When I was in my Night, I had people shun me because they were disappointed in me or angry with me. They would have been shocked if the black fire had prevailed and I had killed myself. They would have attributed it to how sick I was without realizing that the isolation they imposed, in combination with other factors, can be like kerosene on a fire.

It is a black fire. In the black fire, few people will come running toward you. It produces no light on the horizon to alert people that a major loss is occurring. What is it that makes the fire black and makes your self-destructive thinking invisible?

The answer is simple: shame.

FIVE

The Black Hole of Shame

Astrophysicists tell us that when a large star collapses in upon itself, the gravitational field becomes so large that even light cannot escape its pull. At the moment it crosses that threshold, it disappears from the night sky. The internal forces turning it inward have rendered it invisible. It becomes a black hole.

It you sat on the surface of the body in the center of a black hole and radioed for help, your signal would never reach a potential rescuer. It would curve back toward you in an inescapable arc. You would be alone with yourself.

Shame can be so powerful in our lives that it effectively shuts down all signals to the outside world about what is really happening to you. It makes you invisible. Why is it that people in the Night of suicidal thinking are watching the black fire destroy their Soul and can't call out for help? If our houses were on fire, we would not hesitate to call the fire department to come save our possessions. Are our lives worth less than our sticks of furniture?

Jesus once asked an important question, "What shall a man give in exchange for his soul?" (Matthew 16:26 KJ21). What would you give in exchange for your Soul? Shame about suicide renders the Soul practically worthless. I'd call the fire department if my house catches on fire. I'd call a plumber if my toilet overflows. But I won't call for help when I am thinking about killing myself! Shame has so distorted my values that my toilet is more important than my life! Think about it.

Families also allow themselves to be engulfed in the black hole of shame. To have a family member who has attempted or died by suicide is a source of great embarrassment for many. Even admitting that someone in your family is thinking about suicide is shameful.

Most people lost in the wilds die of shame.
Most Hansels and Gretels are so busy blaming
themselves for getting lost in the first place
that they don't do the one thing needed to survive:
think about what to do next.

She had rehearsed it all in her mind. On cue, at 2:00 a.m. that night, she arose from her bed, pulled on her robe and slippers, and walked out of the house while her husband and children lay sleeping. She left no note. The stream she journeyed toward was a good mile from the house, a difficult trek through fields and pastures even for a fully-dressed and healthy person, let alone a woman with a chronic and debilitating heart condition. Nonetheless, she pressed forward, driven by a resolve that she could no longer allow the burden of her poor health to fall on the shoulders of her loved ones.

Whether aided by moon or starlight we do not know, but she persevered through the darkness to stand at the water's edge. With the same determination that had led her from house to stream, she shook off her robe and slippers for the last time, leaving them for the unlucky discoverers to spot and claim. She waded into the water and, after a few steps, turned so as to be walking backwards. The water was above her knees. "Deep enough now," she thought. Then, she let her body glide backwards and her head drop below the water covering her face. She was drowning herself. The woman's name was Mattie Waddell. She was my grandmother.

No one would know the story were it not for the fact that her daughter, my mother, found the slippers the next day . . . beside her mother's bed.

"Mommy, why are your slippers all muddy?" she asked.

As far we know, my mother was the only person with whom my grandmother shared what had happened the night before. She related the desperate sojourn through the darkness, the long walk across fields, the sad purpose that drove her, and the descent into the water. Then, she added this, "As my head went back and I began to take in the water, I felt a hand beneath my head, lifting it up. I believe it was the hand of God. I believe he was telling me that it was not my time to die." She told how she had risen from the water, donned her robe and slippers, and walked home. She died several years later of natural causes. What I find so remarkable about this story is that I did not hear it until I was sixty years old. (This story was not in the first edition of this book. It was not until my mother read my story that she told me about my grandmother.)

A number of years ago, I was scheduled to speak at a conference on mental health and spirituality. On the day I was scheduled to speak, the phone rang early in the morning. It was a family member who had heard I was speaking at the conference. The person was quite angry.

"You're not going to tell them you've been thinking about suicide, are you? That would reflect badly on our whole family."

Shame totally reverses our scale of values. We become more concerned about how we appear to others than the true state of our Soul. What is of little relative importance in the big picture becomes overwhelming. What is of great importance is given little regard. It happens to all of us. However, if we are going to be finally liberated we must reestablish our Soul as having the greatest value of our lives.

Shame is not guilt. Guilt is the actual failure to comply with a moral, ethical, or spiritual law. Shame is the self-condemnation that arises from failing the standard we set for one's self or the standard set for us by other people. It is possible to feel great shame and not be guilty at all! Because so much of our shame is religion-based, I want to address it with two stories in the Bible.

There is a story in the New Testament about a woman who had been hemorrhaging for twelve years. She had gone from physician to physician but her condition only worsened. Finally, she decided to make her way to Jesus and touch his clothes. She was healed.

But physical healing, wonderful though it be, is not what this story is finally about. Jesus, sensing a power shift in his own Soul, calls the woman out of the anonymous crowd. She cowers before him. Why? Because she is ashamed of her unclean condition, a shame that is amplified by the crowd around her. The crowd would have been appalled by her behavior. But, is she guilty? Absolutely not! Jesus not only refuses to condemn her, he commends her for her faith. And what is faith in this situation? It is refusing to let shame win.

Shame is often wordless, marked more by silence than outright condemnation. It is absorbed through the pores in a social situation. When a subject is shameful in a culture, a change of subject, a knitted brow, a looking away is a powerful conveyer of the message. One speaker on the subject of suicide described the experience as "hearing crickets" at the end of her speech. In the crowd surrounding this woman, there would have been many furtive thoughts judging her for her conduct. "What does she think she is doing? Does she have no regard for common decency?"

Notice what Jesus does. He takes the woman who is ashamed and heals her. Imagine the consternation of the crowd who just moments before were judging her behavior as highly inappropriate.

The compassionate behavior of Jesus toward the woman requires each person to revaluate his or her attitude. While the woman is relieved of her shame, the people in the crowd who would shame her are left feeling guilty. To shame another person so that he or she is prevented from finding needed healing is true guilt—it it is a violation of God's gracious love. By reversing the order of things, Jesus restores the woman back to her rightful concern, not what the crowd thinks of her, but the value of her own life.

Take another biblical story, the account of Bartimaeus. Because it is less familiar I will quote it below.

> Then they came to Jericho. As Jesus and his disciples, together with a large crowd, were leaving the city, a blind man, Bartimaeus (that is, the Son of Timaeus), was sitting by the roadside begging. When he heard that it was Jesus of Nazareth, he began to shout, "Jesus, Son of David, have mercy on me!" Many rebuked him and told him to be quiet, but he shouted all the more, "Son of David, have mercy on me!" Jesus stopped and said, "Call him." So they called to the blind man, "Cheer up! On your feet! He's calling you." Throwing his cloak aside, he jumped to his feet and came to Jesus. "What do you want me to do for you?" Jesus asked him. The blind man said, "Rabbi, I want to see." "Go," said Jesus, "your faith has healed you." Immediately he received his sight and followed Jesus along the road (Mark 10:46-52 NIV).

Notice what is happening here. Bartimaeus is a blind man who has been reduced to begging. The fact that his father is mentioned means that this man is known in the community. When he hears that Jesus is near, he begins to call out for help. The crowd shames him and tries to get him to keep quiet. But like the woman with the hemorrhage, he refuses to let the crowd imprison him. Again, Jesus not only refuses to shame Bartimaeus, he affirms his faith, which is demonstrated in his refusal to let shame win. The people in the crowd, on the other hand, the ones that tried to shame Bartimaeus into keeping quiet are now required to reevaluate their attitude. Each person has to ask, "What does it means that I was so ready to shame a man into silence that Jesus was so willing to help?" Jesus takes the man who was shamed and frees him. He takes the people in the crowd who would shame him and leaves them guilty.

If you are in the Night of suicidal thinking and you are reading this book in search of an answer, please take note. There is something very right about you and something quite wrong about a society that shames you into silence. The miracle of God's grace that I pray is dawning upon you as you read these words is that a great reversal is taking place in your thinking. God elevates you as a person who steps out of the shadow of shame, and he judges those who would shame you. The last becomes first, the first, last.

There is a dream
and there is a fear.
They writhe on the floor of the Soul
in mortal combat
as the village sleeps,
not knowing,
that the morning,
and a thousand mornings,
hangs on a button of hope.

Deliverance from the shame of suicidal thinking requires shifting the guilt back to the community and out of your own Soul. The human race needs to deal with the reality that we have created societies so toxic to hope and relationships that certain members perceive their only option is to kill themself. This is the dark secret of human society: The most frequent cause of violent death in the world is not the war or murder, which we see on the front pages of our newspapers. More people kill themselves than are killed by murder or war! If we keep it quiet, the reality is denied. This is society's shameful reaction to the uncomfortable truth. In this way, society becomes guilty.

Suicide is a uniquely human act. It is not a natural impulse. The suicidal person must absorb the hopelessness and sense of isolation from the communities that shape us. Some societies are much more toxic than others. When suicide rates across the globe are examined they reveal that some nations have suicide rates that are seventy-five times higher than the communities with the lowest rates. Many Latin American countries have remarkably low rates of suicide. You are five times more likely to kill yourself if you live in the United States than you would be if you were born and raised, for example, in Paraguay. This is true in spite of the fact that the standard of living in Paraguay is roughly a tenth of what it is in the United States.

During the late 1990s I was traveling back and forth to Honduras to start a project for children with HIV. The World Health Organization reports that Honduras has no suicides. While there is clearly an issue with under reporting, I have to say that I encountered considerable astonishment from ordinary Hondurans that the teenagers and young adults in the United States are killing themselves at such a high rate. One high school teacher in a bilingual school indicated that he did not know of a single case of a suicide of a high school student. When I asked him why he thought Honduran students were less likely to kill themselves, he indicated that in his school, the children were considered to be a part of his family, a family that produced an environment in which they knew they belonged.

In contrast to my Honduran friend's reflection that focused on the community as a way of understanding suicide, people in the United States tend to think differently about it. The incidence of suicide is generally linked to factors within the individual, either character flaws such as selfishness, cowardice, sin, and so forth or mental illnesses such as depression, bipolar disorder, and schizophrenia. There is no question that individual factors play a role in suicidal thinking. But the truth is that most people dealing with these issues do not suicide. There is a community dimension to suicide as well.

Think about cholera. There are parts of the world that have much higher cholera death rates than others. While the disease is contracted through an individual behavior (eating contaminated food or drinking contaminated water), the issue is addressed as a problem in the community. The World Health Organization takes this approach when it states, "cholera is mainly transmitted through contaminated water and food and is closely linked to inadequate environmental management."

Jesus said it well:
The hero of today was the villain of yesterday.
Treat the voices around you as you might a radio station:
Sometimes up.
Sometimes down.
Sometimes off.

What would happen if we understood the stark differences in the rates of suicide from one community to another as a problem in the way a community managed its life? It would be truly radical to read: "Suicide is the intentional taking of one's own life occuring particularly in communities that isolate people by shunning, marginalizing, ignoring, or ridiculing and deprive them of hope by denying them opportunities for growth, development, personal expression, and productive work."

Because the institutions that comprise our communities—schools, churches, neighborhoods, businesses, families, and health care—find it difficult to face the tough question of why we are creating a society in which people feel so desperate, the shame is shifted to the individual. We focus on the illness or inadequacy of the person. While a shift from the flawed character model (cowardice, sin, selfishness) to an illness model (mental illness, for example, depression, irrationality, distorted thinking) promises a more compassionate approach, it still traumatizes the individuals by leaving them with the impression that suicidal thinking is uncommon, that only sick people think about suicide, and that the community in which they live bears no responsibility for the fact that so many people are killing themselves, attempting to kill themselves, or thinking about killing themselves.

Suicidal thinking is considered shameful by most of us. That shame causes people in the Night to black-hole their suicidal thinking. They become preoccupied with fear of what others may think. They stop communicating what is happening to others. Shame preoccupies people in the Night with less important matters (like what people think), distorts their values, and places their precious life at risk. The grace of God reverses this process by lifting the shamed into healing and acceptance while rendering guilty those who shame others. Communities play a role in spreading the hopelessness and isolation that spawns and exacerbates suicidal thinking. If people in the Night of suicidal thinking are to step out of the black hole of shame they must allow their communities to bear their own shame rather than incorporating it into their Soul.

The Missing Sacrament

Shake the dust off your feet.
Do not carry the shame of failure
Into the next town of your work,
Lest a former work contaminate a new one.

Shame of failure can slay a Soul.
Don't ask forgiveness for your shame!
It cannot be forgiven away
or repented away.
Like a venomous viper
it can only be shaken off,
between conversations,
or moments of giving,
or from one day to the next.

Shaking off the dust of shame
is permission to quit the past
to say enough is enough,
to quit outwardly but inwardly as well,
to let the mind stop
its processing of what could have been
In preference for yet can be.

Honoring Our Soul

arly in his epic poem "The Divine Comedy," the Italian poet Dante Alighieri describes a situation "so terrible it is that death is hardly worse" (Tant'è amara che poco è più morte). Most of us have concluded a conversation about tragic circumstances of one sort or another with a similar sentence: "There are some things worse than death." The New Testament also speaks of situations in which people find "[hoping for death] less agonizing than living life" (Revelation 9:6 CEV). This is an ancient and common experience for human beings. For example, fleeing from Jezebel, Elijah sits down under a tree and prays, "I have had enough, Lord, . . . Take my life" (1 Kings 19:4 NIV).

So what is it that Dante finds so painful? A degenerative, medical condition threatening to rob him of the human qualities of thought and speech? A life-shattering accident leaving him paralyzed and helpless? An abusive situation in which he was being imprisoned or tortured? It is none of these. Dante is wrestling with an issue characteristic of midlife: his Soul. At the time of writing, Dante was thirty-five years of age, half of the traditional threescore years and ten.

Here is how he describes it: "In the middle of the journey of our life I came to my senses in a dark forest, for I had lost the straight path."

The poet David Whyte describes this experience as coming to the realization that we cannot keep telling the same story any longer because the story is patently untrue. Perhaps it has never been true, but we felt we had to tell the story anyhow. The realization that the story is untrue feels like coming to your senses in a dark forest, dense, wild, and tangled.

It is the untangling process that seems most daunting. What you are untangling will often seem like a further tangling to others. This is simply another way of saying that at the very moment you are coming closer to some authentic life within your being, it will appear to others that you are simply messing up your life.

When living your life in truth in a way that honors your Soul feels worse than death, death feels like a better option than living. That process is the incubator of suicidal thinking. That thinking does not stop simply because someone wants it to.

As we observed earlier, it would be great if we could just say, "Stop it!" to people thinking about suicide and bring it to a halt. If you are a First Day person you understandably may think the solution is this easy. Of course, the easiest way to get people to think about anything is to tell them not to think about it. Don't think "turkey." You already have the gobbler in your head. You have to think about it in order to decide not to think about it. But there is more to the problem of suicidal thinking than that.

The most important matters of our lives are not subject to brute command. We do not fall in love on command, nor do we fall asleep on command. We can't command happiness. Or joy. Or serenity. Neither can we deliver ourselves from our stronger demons on command. The forceful pulling of the undesirable weeds from our character destroys the flowers of beauty and goodness we want to save. We cannot be scolded out of killing ourselves.

To stop thinking about suicide, you have to first change the part of you that began thinking about suicide in the first place.

It is no surprise for most persons to learn that human beings often cannot bear to let go of the very things that are killing them. We are now aware of the power of addictive substances and stimuli. Many of these are killers. Alcoholism, as an example, is a fatal disease. Most people understand, to one degree or another, the dangers associated with addiction, and they adopt the conventional wisdom of trying to steer clear of them. Most are successful.

For those of us already thinking about suicide, addictive behaviors can deepen the Night of suicidal thinking and ramp up its dangers. They increase our isolation by encouraging behaviors that make it more difficult for people to be in relationship with us. Isolation almost always increases risk. In addition, addictive behaviors can reduce our inhibitions and impair our judgment, making a suicide easier for us to attempt.

In a nutshell, addictions are bad for us. They can become more deadly if we are thinking about suicide. But even if we tell ourselves to stop thinking about suicide, and we avoid drugs and alcohol, it still may not be enough to save us.

My wife is an emergency nurse working in a pediatric hospital. She says that when a child comes in holding his or her wrist, it's a mistake to assume that the injury is located at the place the child is holding. Usually the child is stabilizing the arm in order to keep the injured part from moving because movement causes pain. For many people in the Night, suicidal thinking is a way of avoiding movement, specifically, the liberation of the Soul to its fullest expression.

Every person has a Soul. The Soul is not an ethereal ghost that finally abandons the body and shoots off to heaven when we die.

The Soul is that central thrust of your life to become something or do something that connects you to the vibrancy of life and living. For some the Soul drives toward the healing arts, for others writing and poetry, for still others research and discovery. Like love, it is a many-splendored thing.

Last year I went to a flintknappers convention near Flint Ridge, Ohio. Flint Ridge boasts one of the largest accessible deposits of flint in the United States. The flint is of such high quality that the Native Americans east of the Mississippi made the area a no-conflict zone to ensure that everyone had access to the raw materials necessary for fashioning the hunting tools essential for survival.

Flintknapping is an art that requires years to learn. For many, it is clearly a calling of the Soul. One flintknapper was also an auto-body mechanic. He compared turning a piece of flint into an arrowhead to the restoration of a badly wrecked car. "In both cases," he said, "you have to contemplate it in silence until 'something' tells you how to proceed." This man has a Soul that must contemplate, conceive, and shape the minerals of the earth. It is as deep and profound as any call to priesthood or other religious office. The same is true for everyone. Everyone has a Soul.

The Soul is always striving for integrity. It is seeking to find a way to express what is consistent with its own experience and true to its sense of purpose. A Soul is free. It cannot be bought or sold. It should not be coerced or controlled.

There is no greater mythic tribute to the integrity of the Soul than the temptation of Jesus. Raised by a carpenter father to become a carpenter, Jesus decides in his late twenties that his Soul requires him to move in a different direction. He becomes an itinerate preacher. No one in his family supports this decision. Most people in his hometown ridicule him. The crisis is crystallized in the story of his sojourn in the wilderness. There he is met by Satan who invites him to abandon his Soul and its mission. Satan tempts him to self-doubt ("if you are the Son of God"), to be preoccupied with what others think of him (casting himself down from a public place so that people could see angels "lift [him] up in their hands"), and finally to define himself in terms of power and position ("I will give you all their authority and splendor [kingdoms of the world]" Luke 4:3, 11, 6 NIV).

Society will always be able to make more money on your shame, your fear, and your inadequacy than it can on your wholeness, peace, and aspirations. The primary thrust of most marketing efforts is to first create dissatisfaction with your life and yourself. At their darkest, the communities of which we are a part often resist the development of a rich and robust Soul. I have even seen church members infuriated when a well-known and poorly regarded member of the congregation begins to honor his own Soul and find a rich, meaningful life. In the biblical story often referred to as the parable of the prodigal son, it is the prodigal's own brother who cannot deal with the fact that the son has finally "come to himself."

Growth of our Soul often creates painful reactions on the part of our families and communities. When movement causes pain, we may stop moving, and when we stop moving, we stop growing. Like a child coming into a hospital emergency room, we try to hold ourselves still to avoid pain. As communities, we give one another subtle but powerful messages that change is not acceptable. I am not referring only to changes that turn us into criminals and pose the threat of bodily harm or emotional abuse. Growth in unexpected directions, however positive, can feel threatening also.

> Do not flirt with having a Soul while
> married to the status quo.
> The status quo will never divorce you quietly;
> it will sue you for every penny.

A number of years ago, I developed a list of twenty signs of a robust and growing Soul. I list them below. Ponder each one.

1. Are you increasingly alert to messages you are receiving from the universe—the coincidences, synchronicities, and chance occurrences that favor a course of action not previously planned?

2. Are you willing to risk journeys of discovery, to physically leave the familiar behind and travel without a clear destination?

3. Are you willing to make vocational changes in your life if another path will lead to greater vitality and purpose even at the cost of some security?

4. Though fully aware of religious traditions, do you increasingly honor the discoveries of your own heart and mind, even when they are at odds with commonly-held views? Evidence of growth in this area is that you increasingly speak from the authority of your own experiences rather than always quoting others.

5. Do people increasingly walk away from you feeling energized, stronger, healthier, and better equipped for life?

6. Are you finding a resonant and functional community that honors who you are? This may also require that you be able to walk away from communities that cannot accept what you have to give or are toxic to you even if they are members of your biological family.

7. Do you increasingly recognize self-doubt as an obstacle to change and a predictable temptation to stagnation rather than growth so that you can marshal your spiritual resources to overcome self-doubt rather than surrender to it?

8. Can you accept the desertion or even betrayal of some who are close to you as a predictable element of the spiritual journey without becoming distracted or bitter?

9. Are you avoiding measures that coerce or manipulate people? Spiritually vital persons fascinate or love persons onto a better path. They model for others a full, vital, and growing Soul instead of trying to talk others into changing their behaviors.

10. Are you finding in yourself a growing resilience—capacity to "bounce back" from difficulty? This means refusing to use mood-altering drugs, alcohol, narcotics, or antidepressants as a substitute for making necessary though painful changes to your life.

11. Are you increasingly aware that your beliefs shape your experience? One example of this is taking some time each day to "create" the day ahead that you believe you are supposed to have.

12. Are you increasingly engaged in sensory experience and the fullness of each moment? People who are fully engaged feel the air moving into their lungs as they breathe. They taste their food. They pay attention to the sensations in their bodies.

13. Do you regularly have experiences of "oneness" where you realize your deep connections to all people and things? This may feel like you are flowing into other people as you look at them. Or you may find yourself so intently engaged in something so important that "time stands still."

14. Are you increasingly able to frame the faults of others as strategies that might have worked for them in other times and places but not here and now? This helps you more readily see the assets and potential in people rather than their deficits.

15. Do you increasingly experience God, not only in religious settings, but in all fields of knowledge, all kinds of experiences and all human endeavors?

16. Are you increasingly vulnerable to the joys and sorrows of loving others? When you are growing in this area you find yourself able to risk caring even at the risk of loss. You can tell

someone that you need or miss them. You increasingly resist the temptation to isolate yourself when you feel wounded.

17. Are you increasingly self-aware of your gifts and driving passions as well as the shadows in your life that always threaten to trip you up?

18. Do you have goals for your life that you are moving toward rather than just marking time? Do you have a worthy goal for the next seven days of your precious life?

19. Are you more inclined to take action on important matters in your life rather than become overwhelmed by fear or stuck feeling like a victim? People who are growing in this area resist reciting the same basic storyline over and over with different characters. They are living new stories from those they were living a year ago. They have stopped being surprised over and over by the same basic situations.

20. Are you increasingly able to keep your life in perspective? People who are growing are able to avoid "catastrophizing" the day's events. They can imagine how things might get better. Even if the worst happens they see how they can work creatively with God's help to do something important.

Go back over the list one more time. Think about each one of these in concrete ways. How would the people in your community, your family, your friends, your spiritual community, or persons in your workplace react if you took these seriously? Just how painful would it be? How many relationships would you lose? What might you gain? Would you keep going or would you stop honoring your Soul?

SEVEN

Soul-bleed

hen you stop honoring your Soul, you develop what I call a soul-bleed. When a person is anemic, the first thing my medically-trained wife looks for are the signs of an internal bleed. Other sicknesses result from the attack of an invader, either foreign to the body (bacterial, viral, fungal, chemical) or internal to the body (tumor, auto-immune disorder). But an internal bleed is a sickness of loss. It is invisible to the eye; no red-sopped wound is apparent that would trigger an effort to stem the flow. Yet, something essential to life and vitality is slowly slipping away on the inside.

A soul-bleed occurs when you feel forced to ignore your own life experience, mental states, and needs in order to adapt to the relationships that form your world: family, friendships, career, and spiritual communities. When this happens an internal gap is opened up between the story of your life and the storyline you are telling and living. If unacknowledged, this gap becomes an internal wound that bleeds out, first your zest for living and finally your desire to live at all.

I remember a time when I instinctively used the language of the bleeding Soul with a group, years before I had the clarity that I have today. It was a training situation on the topic of suicide intervention. We were talking about the various resources that a suicidal person may have that might help keep them alive. At that time I was in the process of going through a divorce and had lost the relationship I had with all four of my children.

Children represent the continuation of a long-term relationship and serve as a source of hope and connection for a parent who is thinking about suicide. For women going through a divorce, children provide a protective factor because the relationship with their children usually continues uninterrupted. For men going through a divorce, the relationship with children is often lost. Instead of providing a reason for living, children represent a loss that may accelerate suicidal thinking. What women experience as a reason for living, men may experience as a reason to die.

If you long for a spirituality that brings you the exuberance of living, you have to be willing to disbelieve everything you've been told. If you simply want the comfort of fitting in, just about any belief will do.

I was the only male in the group. I sat there and listened as the women in the group responded to scenario after scenario with the same question: "Do you have children?" If the answer was yes, they proceeded to build their intervention strategy around the children. I felt myself growing physically weaker and somewhat nauseous. I began to attack myself internally: "What was wrong with me that I did not see it the way that they did?" I have come to recognize this question as my standard MO (method of operation) when faced with group behavior that is not consistent with my own thinking or experience; I find a way to ignore my own Soul so that I can fit in. This time it would be different. After the conversation had gone on for about an hour, I could take it no longer.

"I need you all to understand that I feel like I am bleeding out of a hole inside. You keep assuming that children remain in relationship with you during a divorce. That is not my experience! I am finding it very difficult to sit here and listen to you say that over and over again."

I felt like I was throwing myself open to exile from the group, but they acknowledged what I said without any defensiveness at all. They honored my experience by exploring it further, asking questions, and offering understanding. Finally, they thanked me. They told me that my honesty had provided them with a learning experience that would prove useful in their work with men in the future.

With that, I felt something that I can only describe as a healing. My strength returned. The gap between my experience and the relationship with the group closed. My soul-bleed had been stemmed. It was a good beginning.

Any time you feel it necessary to live or think in a way that stands in stark contrast to your life experience, your way of thinking, or your needs as a human being, you are vulnerable to a soul-bleed. Doesn't everyone have to make adjustments to the needs of others? The answer has to be "Yes." But the finest of spiritual teaching acknowledges that we cannot lose ourselves in the process. In the parable of the prodigal son, the text does not describe the moment of the son's insight as giving up his self, but "coming to himself" (Luke 15:17 DBY). Even the oft ascetic-sounding Paul urges balance when he counsels that each man should "not only look after his own interests, but also the interest of others" (Philippians 2:4 ESV).

Everyone must give up some of his or own needs for the sake of a larger community, but in spirituality, psychology, and even science, there seems to be a breaking point.

In the twentieth century, physicists learned about threshold phenomena. These phenomena do not exist below a set point called a threshold; they do not increase gradually. They skip the middle. It would be like pressing down on the accelerator of your car and having nothing happen until suddenly the car jumps instantaneously from zero to fifty miles per hour. Odd as this may sound, every computer, cell phone, and radio could not operate were it not for this threshold phenomena. Perhaps we can adapt to social situations that are not reflective of our own experiences—up to a point. But there is a threshold that we cross to our own harm. We adapt and adapt with little apparent effect, but at some point we realize that we have crossed some unmarked threshold. We have lost ourselves. Afterwards we are no longer at home in our own mind. We have so forsaken and wounded the Soul that many of us begin to self-destruct.

We are born into conformity.
We are aged into peculiarity.

I am neither a psychologist nor a neurobiologist. What is apparent to me is that I clearly overestimated my ability to adapt. I exceeded my self-destructive threshold long ago. There was just too much in my experience and thinking that had to be ignored, unacknowledged, disallowed, or forgotten. By the time I realized what was happening I was already thinking about suicide, and I could not get myself to stop.

A soul-bleed is experienced in different ways. The experiences that you may be required to ignore, disallow, or forget are different from mine.

Sometimes the experiences that we must ignore are those gleaned from our own learning and growth. I remember attending a gathering of clergy at a mid-career conference. These were folks who had been ordained for fifteen years or more. I was struck by the impression that not one person spoke as if they had changed their mind on anything significant over the entire span of their ministry. Those who had begun as theological conservatives were still conservatives. Those who had begun as theological liberals were still liberals.

There was one exception. In the middle of the meeting when a modicum of trust had begun to loosen tongues, one man made a remarkable confession:

> I spent most of my years serving a church in Texas. I was known for my conservative theology. I fought gay ordination at every turn. I led my Presbytery in passing a resolution on the issue to send to the General Assembly. Two years ago, I moved to serve a church in Ohio. Shortly after the move, I discovered that my only brother had AIDS, and that he was gay. I cried. I prayed. I bargained. But eventually I buried my brother.
>
> After his death, I rethought everything. I went back to the Scriptures. I studied. I listened. And at the end of that process, I changed my views. Now I need to tell you this: I am a man without a country. The people on the more liberal side of the church do not trust me. My former colleagues on the conservative side of the church feel betrayed by me. I have lost any sense of community.

It was as if every voice was paralyzed into silence. I can't read minds, but I would guess that the silence was a fearful one. Every person in the circle was possessed of the sober realization that if any of them had gone through a similar "learning" they also would be a "Man without a Country" (Edward Everett Hale, *The Atlantic*, December 1863). One would wish this were not the case in spiritual communities.

It begins with the fear of disapproval.
Then comes the fear of exclusion.
Then the fear of losing your lifestyle.
Then your job.
Then your health.
Then your safety.
Then you fear losing life itself.
Finally you are a slave who has lost every ounce of freedom
    and it no longer matters if you live or die.

How far are you willing to go to maintain the favor of your community when you have good reason to believe the community can reject you without a quiver of conscience? How long can you justify your silence as the better part of valor? At what point have you passed the threshold of your own capacity to make yourself fit? When does your Soul begin to bleed out your zeal for living and eventually begin to self-destruct?

Sometimes the experience that we feel must go unacknowledged, denied, or ignored is the destructiveness of a relationship, often an intimate one. Twenty-five percent of the women who kill themselves in the Night of their suicidal thinking are being abused by an intimate partner. Many women who are now in their Second Day had to decide that their Souls were worth more than their familiar, yet abusive relationships.

Less obvious to us may be the soul-bleed that is caused when we are in an intimate relationship that has died, but we cannot acknowledge that death. Shortly after the separation from my wife and my resignation from the church, I received a call from one of the members asking me to lunch. I wondered if this was going to be another "dressing down."

I met him in a small delicatessen with counters around the windows where the patrons sat as they ate their lunches. He asked me how I was doing and listened to me pour out some pain and anxiety. Finally, he finished his sandwich and pushed the wrapper back to clear a space for his elbow as he turned to square his body with me.

"You know, my marriage is a real struggle," he said. "In fact, there's not much left. There hasn't been for quite a while. There was a time when I was so depressed by it all that I was dangerously suicidal."

"Are you thinking of killing yourself now?" I asked.

"Oh no," he answered. "Not any more. I'm on an antidepressant. As long as I stay on the medication, I'm okay."

"What would happen if you became honest about the state of your marriage and ended it?" I asked. "Would you still need to be on medication?"

"Probably not," he answered. "But I'm a Christian. People at the church would make that difficult for me. I could never do it."

In retrospect, it does not seem that my friend was in a Second Day; he was in a medicated Night. The prospect of the changes required for him to enter a Second Day, the rebuke of his community, and the challenge of starting over alone were just too much.

> Only the touch of a strong man can be gentle.
> A weak man's hand shakes and his errant nails
> will always pierce you.
> His fear will scratch you to death.

I have nothing but compassion for folks in a medicated Night; I spent about two years in a medicated Night myself. I had never experienced clinical depression. In the summer of 1998, depression hit me like a 300-pound linebacker. I had little energy, limited mental focus, and I lost all creativity. I couldn't sleep at night, and I couldn't stay awake during the day. Pep talks were useless. They felt like commands to jump out of a fifteen-foot emotional hole in the ground.

The antidepressant prescribed for me worked like magic. My energy was back along with my focus and creativity. I felt like myself again. Unfortunately I didn't know who "myself" was. Two years later, when I went off the medication, most of the issues that had sent me into depression remained. I had to make a decision. Which is the better choice? Make the changes required to live medication free? Or maintain the status quo and rely on medication to ward off suicidal thinking?

I make no judgment on the answer to that question for others. But I believe that as families, friends, and spiritual communities, we have to be clear about the answer to our side of this question: Would you prefer to have the person that you love avoid major changes in his or her life with the hope that medication would keep them free of suicidal thoughts and relatively happy or would you prefer to have the person that you love free of medication and suicidal thoughts, if it meant that they would be different in significant ways from how you have known them in the past?

For myself, I kept harkening back to the words of Jesus of Nazareth, "What shall a man give in exchange for his Soul?" (Matthew 16:26 KJ21). To reframe the question, "What is worth the bleeding of your Soul? How far are you willing to go in ignoring, denying, and forgetting your own experience, your own thinking, and your own intuitions? What is the sign that you have crossed the threshold? Is it when you find yourself not wanting to get up in the morning? Is it when you find yourself saying, "This job is killing me"? Is it when your creative energy has evaporated and the art is gone from your life? Is it when God has become a doctrine, an idea, a theory, rather than a guiding presence and source of beauty in your life?

In one sense, people in the Night of suicidal thinking have the real advantage of clarity. The decibel level of self-destruction leaves them without a doubt that they have crossed the threshold. Like a child holding one's wrist to keep it from moving, they are holding their life as motionless as possible to avoid the pain of rejection from the community should they choose to change and grow. It feels to them that people would rather have them dead than different.

No one, of course, would ever say that they would rather have you dead than different. Such a declaration would be the equivalent of murder, in this case the killing of the relationship. People usually don't kill relationships with hatred but with indifference. They avoid you, stop calling you, or keep you at arm's length. This is the truth of the zombie mythology. We create populations of people who are the living dead because we refuse to allow them to grow robust and vibrant souls.

People in the Night of suicidal thinking may accurately perceive this reality. Many times I said to my therapist Azaria Akashi that it seemed many people in my life would rather have me dead than different. She never disputed my perception. She did challenge my interpretation of what that meant. For me, it meant that I needed to die. For her, and a number of persons like her, it meant that I needed to be born into a Second Day. These persons are so rare and special that I coined a name for them: Othersouls.

EIGHT

The Othersouls

When the Santa Anna winds drive a red fire through the dry brush of southern California, not much stands between the homes that are destroyed and those that are not. One house stands untouched while on the left and the right only the ashes of other homes remain. The Viking Loki was not only the god of fire, but also the god of mischief and capriciousness. Brush fires are like Loki. No one knows for sure what the fire will level next.

When you are in the Night of the black fire of suicidal thinking, you are struck by how close you pass to others who do not know this fire at all. You walk down the street and pass within a few inches of others who are not thinking about suicide. You begin to wonder what that is like. "What's it like to be you?" you want to ask. "How is it that the black fire is burning down my soul and not yours? What's your secret?"

You become aware of the thin line between thought and action. A simple turn of the wheel of your speeding car is all it would take. You begin to look at trees along the side of the road in a different way. You imagine your car wrapped around them. It can happen so fast. I remember standing at the counter of a department store and trying to buy a gun. Only a few minutes before, I had been taking a nap.

Becoming a new creation is way overrated.
The preacher homilizes as if becoming a new creation
is the best thing since Velcro. Come on!
The last thing in the world people want you to do is really change.
What Republican wants his friend to become a Democrat
or like polo when he used to go to football games?
Who wants the friend who gave him boat rides to sell
his boat and start collecting quarters?
If you want stability, stay a caterpillar.
Butterflies suck at staying put.

When you realize that you can't put the black fire out, that you can't stop thinking about suicide, your remaining option is to try to keep the thought from becoming deed. Life at the firebreak between suicidal thought and suicidal action is hard and lonely. Few people seem to be able to handle the revelation that you are considering suicide. Family members often feel shamed by your thinking. Friends, feeling overwhelmed, may push you further away. You realize that your suicidal thinking, if disclosed, will render you unemployable to a number of businesses. You will never be able to run for public office. In your mind, you see a hallway of doors slamming shut, an image that deepens your hopelessness and only accelerates your self-destructive thinking.

Perhaps all would be lost were it not for the Othersouls. An Othersoul is a person who is able to stand with you on the thin line between suicidal thought and action, and then walk with you into your Second Day, the time when the black fire of suicidal thinking has been extinguished. Othersouls are able to listen to you talk about the black fire, the future you have lost, and the temptation to act. They may be quiet and reflective in their response, allowing you to hear yourself think out loud. Or they may be uncomfortably energetic. One person became angry at the thought that I would leave him. One pounded on my chest in the middle of her office. My daughter simply told me it was unacceptable because I had to walk her down the aisle of her wedding.

> Sometimes the only way of knowing that you are loved is by getting lost and waiting to see if anyone comes looking for you.

Othersouls vary in their response, but they all have one thing in common: love. They make it clear that they want you around for as long as they can have you. They love your Soul enough to accompany you on whatever journey that Soul takes you.

Black-holed people don't tell others that they have seriously considered suicide because they are terrified of discovering that most of the relationships in their lives are highly conditional. Even the most irrational person knows that conditional love is not love at all. When you cannot be honest about who you are, what you believe, whom you love, and what you must do, you begin to twist yourself into a pretzel to keep the hounds of rejection at bay. Many of our communities have a way of turning us into prostitutes of a sort, selling our Souls for the sake of keeping our jobs, our families, and our relationships.

One of the great gifts of suicidal thinking is that it discloses to us the Othersouls in our lives who may not otherwise be obvious to us. An account from the New Testament (Luke 7:36-50 NIV) illustrates one woman's discovery. Jesus is visiting the home of a religious man named Simon. Their dinner is inconveniently interrupted by a woman who has "lived a sinful life." She bursts onto the scene without a shred of propriety. It is a tough room. Simon knows who she is. He believes her life is unredeemable and wishes she were gone. While he would never consciously admit that he wants her dead, Simon's actions to deprive her of hope and social connection poison the apple of life and make suicide more likely.

She fumbles the lid from an alabaster jar of perfume; her hand is shaking and she can't make it stop. Her eyes circle the room only once. The expressions on the faces tell her she has made a big mistake Maybe she has. She wonders, "Why do I keep putting myself in these kinds of situations with people who do not really care for me?" Many of us ask ourselves this question.

She hates crying, but she starts crying. No basin has been offered her. Tears will have to be her only water and hair her only towel as she washes the feet of Jesus and dries them with her hair.

Simon's eyes dart around the room. His suspicions about Jesus have been confirmed. If Jesus were a prophet he would have known that this is a woman who has lived a sinful life. It does not occur to Simon that if Jesus knew what kind of man he was, he might never have entered his house!

At the moment, Simon is not a student of his own Soul. He is focused on the sinful woman. What sins does Simon have in mind? Perhaps she spends most of her life pretending to be someone she is not in order to keep her friends, her family, or her livelihood. Perhaps her "sinful life" means that she has fallen for the most serious spiritual temptation of all, selling her Soul to accommodate the conditional loves in her life. Perhaps her sinful life involves prostituting herself by selling her body. The way our minds "fill in the blank" when a person is simply described as living a sinful life tells us more about ourselves than is does about the "sinner"!

In this tough room with Simon and all those beholden to his point of view, what chance does she have? In fact, her chances of surviving whatever self-destructive thoughts are pulsing through her brain have just risen dramatically because of one person in the room. Here is the truth she has discovered that will drive her, even trembling, into any crowd with a story of hope—one person who loves us can outweigh a hundred who do not.

In his book *The Wounded Healer,* Henri Nouwen writes "Let us not diminish the power of waiting by saying that a lifesaving relationship cannot develop in an hour. One eye movement or one handshake can replace years of friendship when [a person] is in agony. Love not only lasts forever, it needs only a second to come about" (page 67, Doubleday, New York, 1979). In a moment of time, you can save a life.

Sins are common to all people and generally uninteresting. Far more fascinating and revealing are the responses of folks to others whose sins are brought into the light. The woman has broken free from the gravity of her own shame. She has taken a step toward her own integrity. She honored her own Soul, even when it led her to what would appear to be a highly inappropriate act of physical contact with a man.

In the process she discovered that Jesus is an Othersoul. He cares for her Soul. He is more concerned that she be true to her own sense of destiny and purpose than about the propriety of her actions. He loves her unconditionally. Above all else, he does not want to lose her company on the journey of life.

Simon, on the other hand is all that she feared he would be. She always suspected that any move toward her own integrity would be met with shunning and marginalization. She is right. Simon is ready to murder any relationship that does not meet his conditions. People like Simon make suicide more likely.

The woman has discovered something that Simon can never know: she is loved unconditionally. She has discovered an Othersoul. This is a gift she could not have discovered any other way. In contrast, as long as Simon is black-holed by his own shame, he will always have to live with the question: Would I really be loved as the wondrous, yet flawed, human being that I really am?

This is the gift that you receive as a person in the Night. If you can let others know who you are and what is happening to you, you will discover Othersouls who love you without condition. They want you to stay alive, not because it would be shameful for you to kill yourself, but because they would miss you terribly if you did.

Othersouls can't put out the black fire of your suicidal thinking. But they can walk with you on the line between thought and action to help keep you alive until the fire goes out. Sometimes you have to seek them out. Once you find them, you have to let them help you. I went through a time in my life when I was calling my Othersouls on a rotating basis to try to stay alive. I didn't always talk about suicide. But I always knew I could if I needed to.

One important group of Othersouls is that body of people who have both the compassion and the professional training to help those in the Night of suicidal thinking. If you are thinking about killing yourself, it is important that you find a mental health professional who can help you sort out the meaning of your thoughts. Not every counselor is "in your bag." Find someone who feels like a good fit and understands who you are and what is important to you. Most importantly, get started as soon as possible. If you don't feel that you have the energy to locate someone, call the suicide hotline in your community for a referral.

Of course, the same process that reveals the Othersouls in your life will also disclose the Simons—and you may find many more Simons than Othersouls. At this point you must make one of the most important decisions of your existence. At the heart of the universe, what is it more like: Jesus or Simon? Is God more like the unconditionally loving Othersoul who would miss you terribly if you were not in his universe? Or is God more like Simon who is ready to banish you from his life unless you walk his straight and narrow line?

The question is not one settled by simple counting. Gold is all the more precious because it is rare in spite of how much more sand there is on the planet. One Othersoul may tell you more about the universe than a hundred Simons.

It's a strange thing. I realized that I had to find my Othersouls and let them know I needed help. And yet, I have this strange feeling that they found me. I think I know why this is. I believe that the universe was trying to find me and keep me alive. Whether I sought my Othersouls or they sought me, it was all part of one rescue conspiracy. This is what Jesus meant, "You did not choose me, but I chose you" (John 15:16 NIV).

I became aware of this conspiracy through one particular experience. I was going to spend the night in my childhood home. I can't remember the circumstance, except that I knew I was going to be there alone. That worried me. I had already asked my brother to remove from the house the shotguns that I had hunted with as a boy; he had taken them to his home in Cincinnati. I was still anxious about what I might do to myself if left alone in the house. I shared this with Shawn, the woman who was later to become my wife. As a wonderful Othersoul, she asked me to call her that evening so that she could make sure I was safe. I never made the call.

That evening, as I lay down to take a nap, an image formed in my mind. It was a woman's face, one I did not recognize. Her nose was about two inches from my nose. A voice said, "Breathe, Russ. Breathe with me." And I did. I breathed in rhythm with her breathing. Then the voice said, "Don't you leave me." And then again: "Breathe, Russ. Breathe with me."

This went on for a number of minutes, the gentle command to breathe alternating with the stronger command not to leave her (whoever she was). What was striking to me was that I could not turn away from her face; she was literally in my face no matter which way I turned. Finally, after about fifteen minutes, the image faded. But all that evening, whenever I reflected upon what had happened, the face returned, nose to my nose. I had no anxiety for the rest of the evening and slept through the night. At first I didn't share this experience with anyone.

About a week later, Shawn and I were hiking. We stopped to rest by sitting on the trunk of a fallen tree. I decided to share the story with her. "Russ, she said in amazement, "that night, I prayed that God would send an angel to keep you safe through the night! God answered my prayer!" It was then that I knew that the universe was trying to keep me alive.

No matter where you go,
a miracle will always be tugging at your sleeve
if you will only turn your head to see it.

I believe the universe is trying to keep all of us alive until we have learned the lessons we need to learn. Sometimes the black fire is too strong, the pain is too great, the desperation too deep, and the perception of love too weak to hold the line between suicidal thought and suicidal action. When a person suicides, the entire universe must shift to a new purpose—healing the person who has died in another dimension with Othersouls who exist only in that dimension. One way or another, the lessons must be learned. In addition the universe now sends Othersouls to the survivors left behind who are now at risk for the black fire to ignite from the sparks of pain that have fallen in their own souls. These are the survivors of suicide.

I wish I could say that the experience of the angel extinguished the black fire of my own suicidal thinking. It did not. But I began to realize that I had Othersouls on both sides trying to help me.

The Night of suicidal thinking had given me a great gift. The universe was more like Jesus than it was like Simon. I had always cognitively believed this. Now, I knew it with certainty.

I was beginning to have hope. I was headed into my Second Day.

NINE

Dawn

I love the word *two* (don't you?). I think it is the shyness of the "w" secretly holding the ends of the word in connection. It is a sacred reminder of all the invisible forces that support and hold things together, from the magnet on your refrigerator, to the love that threads one heart to another. The invisibly real has an unspeakable beauty. When we comprehend the invisible, we know more than we can say.

How appropriate that the deliverance from darkness begins with twilight, which means literally "two-lights"—the moon which is light of the Night and the sun which is light of the day. In the twilight you are between the Night's almost irresistible pull to destroy yourself and the Second Day's exuberant burst into living anew. In the twilight you are finally freed from the insistent voice of death litigating its case inside your skull. There is silence.

I write this in a free-trade coffee shop in an older part of the city. Tomorrow is the Day of the Dead. Strings of black paper with skeleton cutouts are draped from the ceiling. During this ancient Native American celebration, food is offered up for the spirits of those who have died. The spirits eat the "spiritual essence" of the food, leaving what is left for family members (who are still alive in this world) to consume. However, the food has no nutritional value; the spirits have already taken that.

If we get beneath the raucous surface of such celebrations with their indulgence and excess, we often discover a profound truth that we intuit in our souls. Death is the pathway to life. For those who have sojourned in the depths of the Night of suicidal thinking, we have longed to die in order to find release from the pain of this life and to enter into a new one. There is a deep wisdom that has been guiding us all along. Something did need to die in our lives, but it was not us.

I remember a hospital call I made a number of years ago. The church secretary had received a request for the pastor to visit Joanne Miller who was in the hospital. When I left the church I absentmindedly left the note in my office, but thought I remembered the details. I drove to the hospital, went to the information desk in the lobby, and obtained Ms. Miller's room number. At the door I announced myself and indicated I was looking for Joanne Miller. Perplexed, the lady in the bed answered, "Well, I am Joanne Miller, but I am not connected to your church." I apologized and began to back out of the door, when she said, "Would you please come in and talk with me a moment?" When she continued, her words raised goose bumps all over my body. "I have just been told I have three weeks to live. Would you please pray with me?"

As it turned out, I had the correct name, but the wrong hospital. I had it right; I had it wrong. That's the way it is with the Soul. There is a wisdom that we carry. It is right. It is beautiful. It is the pathway to life. But we can make mistakes in how that wisdom is applied to our lives. Many of us who are living a Second Day realize we were right that something needed to die, but wrong about our need to die. Our wisdom was right; our impulse was wrong. Something did need to die; but it was not us.

When what you want becomes impossible, what you create begins.

We each carry an innate wisdom that emanates from our Soul regarding what is needed for us to thrive as spiritual beings. This wisdom is a drive toward vitality, security, and freedom. Vitality is the capacity to engage life fully with emotional zest. Security is a sense of the ultimate good will of the universe toward life. Freedom is the capacity to act unimpeded by inner obstacles such as fear and hate.

When we are soul-sick, it is often because we have denied our inner wisdom for so long that we begin to develop impulses that are distorted responses to that wisdom. When a spiritual source of vitality, security, and freedom is absent, some of us develop an impulse toward chemicals that serve as a substitute. We might call this a chemical spirituality. Chemicals provide a kind of exhilaration, a sense of being alive. They are always there for you; you have the security of knowing they will not leave you. They temporarily deaden the crippling emotions, guilt, shame, fear, and inadequacy and thereby give a sense of freedom.

However, these are false interpretations of what is being experienced. Chemicals do not make us more vital by allowing engagement in life, but drive a gradual withdrawal from living. Chemicals provide a security that must be purchased at a higher and higher cost. The freedom from crippling emotions provided by chemicals is an illusion. These emotions return with a vengeance after each chemical episode bringing with them a whole new trainload of crippling emotions and setting off a new cycle of chemical use.

The impulse to suicide in the neglected Soul also brings a sense of vitality, security, and freedom. People who exhibit exhilaration after a long season of depression have often discovered that their positive energy is the result of a clear, unambiguous decision to kill themselves. It is one of the classic warning signs and one of the most difficult to identify. There is a security in suicidal thinking. Suicide is always an option. It will never leave you. No one can take it away because it is solely your decision. Suicidal thinking frees you from the cage that has trapped you, a cage with bars constructed of your own longing for integrity and your community's threat of rejection. You might call this suicidal spirituality.

Like chemical addiction, the impulse to suicide is a spiritual disease because it is a false answer to a true spiritual need. Our wisdom is right; our impulse is wrong. That's why it is impossible to write a book about suicide without touching on the deepest issues of life. Healing requires the slow, steady process of developing an authentic spirituality to nourish the Soul and replace the suicidal spirituality that has taken root.

Jesus told the story of a merchant looking for fine pearls. One day, he came across one of great value; he went away and sold everything that he had and bought it. This deceptively simple story carries a profound message for us all, but particularly those in the Night of suicidal thinking.

I do not begrudge the hero of a different parable,
who found a pearl and a way to keep italong with his familiar life.
I bless God for his bounty.

But *my* buddy is this fool of a guy who found the pearl
and wasn't smart enough to figure out another way
to have it than to lose everything else.
I'm just glad he made it into the Bible.

From one standpoint, nothing much has changed at the end of the story. The merchant is no richer or poorer. He has simply exchanged one form of wealth (all he had) for another (the pearl). One assumes he could trade it all back if he wanted to and regain all that he had by selling the pearl. His net worth is the same.

The point of the story is not about a change in his financial status; it is that he has exchanged one form of poverty for another.

At the beginning of the story he is a wealthy man who can live in style. Yet, in another sense, he is a poor man: he longs for something of beauty in his life. He has a poverty of beauty.

Then he discovers something of beauty—the great pearl. There is only one catch; it will cost him everything he has. Now he faces a different kind of poverty. His easy, financially secure life is gone, but now he is rich in beauty. He has the pearl.

When you decide to honor your Soul and let it find expression in all its beauty and wisdom, you may be required to exchange one kind of poverty for another. Your need to maintain the conditional love of those around you has required that you dishonor your Soul, leaving you empty and starved. It is a spiritual poverty. When you begin to honor your Soul, many of those conditional resources and relationships may be spent. But a new beauty, one that is priceless and irreplaceable will begin to emerge in your life. It is the beauty of your Soul.

In one sense, the merchant in Jesus's story killed his life as he had known it. In fact, he may have taken a good hard look in the mirror at one point and concluded that his life was not worth living. His impulse was correct and full of wisdom but it did not mean that he needed to kill himself. Something did need to die but it was not he.

When you have spent months or years thinking about killing yourself, God may be calling you to exchange one form of death for another. Instead of killing yourself, God is calling you to kill the idea that you must sacrifice your Soul in order to be loved. When you begin to honor your Soul and allow the Othersouls to assist you, those in this world and those in the next, a new beauty begins to crystallize within you. A new light begins to dawn.

The process by which God begins to extricate us from suicidal thinking is very different from the legalistic religion that many of us have experienced. The process begins by acknowledging that the possibilities of life toward God always increase as authentic spiritual experiences, however small, are folded into one's life.

I decided early in my process that I would rather have a few beliefs that were deep and authentic than many beliefs that were borrowed from others. One of the reasons I kept a journal during these days was so that I could begin to pay attention to the small insights that God was folding into my thinking.

As people have experiences of authentic spirituality and are offered a different way of thinking about their life, their capacity for further spirituality increases with an eventual break in the suicidal impulse. That's why daily experiences of support groups (gathered Othersouls) are often required. The more of God we experience, the more of God we are able to experience, and the more our lives can become whole.

In order to let go of suicidal thinking, a new path to feeling secure must be found. For me security was not found in the belief that God is in control of every detail of life. Once I realized that seven million children die every year from measles and diarrhea, I could no longer subscribe to the belief that God was in control of everything. But I can believe that God is inexhaustibly patient in recreating possibilities for human growth out of every imaginable situation. When I cannot see those possibilities, it is generally because my thinking has been dimmed by fear. Fear does not allow me to see the infinite number of possibilities that exist in any situation. God always has the next best plan. Always. My trust is not placed in God's control of everything but in God's unlimited and eternal capacity to shift in order to develop love, depth, and beauty in the new situation that has just developed. My faith is not that God has painted the final picture of how life will be. My faith is that God is a master artist and whatever colors are thrown onto the palette something of beauty can emerge.

God does not wipe away tears by making us forget.
God wipes away tears by making us aware.

Trusting does not mean ceasing to act. It means listening for the creative possibilities in every situation and refusing to let fear control or close down options. Trust requires that you be present to the moment and releases you to discover the possibility in every situation. It means connecting to the world around you, the realm of nature, the gift of friendship, the direct experience of God in meditation. Trust creates space to focus on the spiritual nutrients in life.

It is God's loving persuasion, not God's control, that is the pathway toward transformation. It is not following rules. It is following clues. I had to stop insisting on blueprints and start looking for fingerprints, the divine touches on different situations. I filled one journal after another with the insights I was learning by simply listening with an open heart and mind. Each person needs his or her own scripture, the record of one's personal revelation, the heavenly vision to obey.

God's persuasive love releases us to the consequences of our own decisions so that we learn from our victories and grow from our mistakes. A Soul that begins to honor its own wisdom will make many mistakes, and it must own those mistakes. The benefit is that it also owns the lessons learned. I made many mistakes during my Night of suicidal thinking but I began to learn lessons that will stay with me the rest of my life. It is for this reason that I often say to people, only half joking, "I wouldn't recommend my life to anyone, but I wouldn't have missed it for the world." I would not be able to say this were it not for the love of God that does not control or punish but patiently and persuasively draws us to the next best plan for our lives.

God's persuasive love can take the form of a steadfast love expressed through an Othersoul that sustains us in the face of rejection. Or it can take the form of a spiritually rich person who simply lives out his or her life in the presence of a suicidal person. The presence of a spiritually rich person in the life of another increases the spiritual possibilities in both lives.

Morning dawns slowly. I remember having several months of consecutively bad days. Then one day I had three hours when I felt vital, secure, and free. But by the afternoon, it was gone. Two weeks later, I had an entire day. After another month, I was beginning to string several good days together. I began to realize that a major shift had taken place in my life. A new day had dawned. I was in my Second Day.

TEN

The Second Day

I renaeus, an early second-century church father, believed that humanity was created immature and God intended his creatures to take a long time to grow into or assume the divine likeness. Adam and Eve were created as children. The Fall was not a full-blown rebellion but rather a childish spat, a desire to grow up before their time and have everything with immediacy. God comes to us in Christ as an infant to grow up with us. Redemption requires a dismantling of the "false adult" and the willingness to grow up again, this time at the right pace.

Second Day people are required to follow a path very similar to that laid out by Irenaeus. Everything has to be taken apart and put together in a new way—and easy does it! About you lay all the worthy endeavors left in suspended animation by the prospect of an abridged life. Your "tartared" teeth need the pick ax of a dentist. Your blood pressure needs to be checked. Your stacked and unsorted papers need to be filed. Your car needs to be serviced. You need to start saving money for retirement. There are people waiting for you to grow old with them and unborn grandchildren waiting for your smile to beckon them into existence. Oh yes, there is your smile waiting to be smiled in a future that is gradually reappearing out of the mist. And there are thoughts waiting to be thought again, thoughts of the dreaming kind.

None of these will be brought back into life by the simple fact that you have decided not to die. The magic lies in your choice to live, a different matter altogether. When you have made the choice to live the sun has broken the horizon and the Second Day has dawned with the force of Yahweh's command, "Let there be light!" You rise on your two wobbly legs, swallowing hard, hands out for balance trying to find a center that will hold. You have chosen to live. Now the task of surveying the landscape begins.

Some things are wilted and gray. They emerge from the darkness like frostbitten pansies beyond resurrection. Second Day people must accept that the Night has killed some things. Some friendships are not salvageable. For these the Night was just too deep, too long, too painful, and too frightening. Some persons cannot deal with you as the person that walked out of the Night. You will grieve these losses. You may be angry and sad. You will say to yourself, "See I always knew it would be this way if I truly entered into the light of my own life." So? You were right. Your wisdom has correctly intuited that some will not walk with you. Let your own wisdom be enough. Accept your gift.

Any man who takes a journey must forgive those who do not go with him or else he never begins.

In your Second Day you will learn that forgiveness is the sun's sister. Wherever there is light in the Second Day there must also be forgiveness, forgiveness of others and forgiveness of self. This will be easier some days than others. But remember, resentment collapses the universe into a box of slights and blinds you to the rest. Forgiveness opens eyes, and you need your eyes to see the wonder of what is emerging from the darkness.

There are those who are waiting just for you, not the contrived you, not the person who tied an anchor to one's waist and nearly tossed oneself to drowning. Your living eyes looking into their eyes are all that they desire. It will be difficult for you to trust this. It will be difficult for them to trust that you have chosen to live. Be patient. The same Night that nearly took you, nearly took you away from them as well. Just as you needed time to emerge from the Night, they must be given time to emerge as well. One of the marks of a living thing is that you cannot make it grow faster. Roses bloom on their own schedule.

The Second Day is not the First Day lived a second time. It is a different day and you will experience it differently. You may find yourself more spiritual and less religious, especially if you experienced religion as indifferent to your Soul. You might discover that you are not strong enough to resist playing to the gallery when you are formally connected to a church or synagogue. Some doctrines you once debated hotly become meaningless to you. Other doctrines take on a depth and reality that you have not known in your most pious First Day moments. Some of your more religious friends may conclude that you have lost the faith. This will seem odd to you. From your experience, God is now as close as your heartbeat. So be it. In the Second Day, you will find the light of God in whatever you follow with passion and love.

Second Day people often reject the previous limitations and role playing that many First Day People find normal and satisfying. It may be difficult for First Day people to understand that an overdose of role playing is your devil's brew. Accept them where they are and withhold easy judgments. Their "normalcy" provides them with a stability that nourished you in your Night. Do not try to take from others what gives them stability and strength. Heartily bless them and then leap into whatever wild wood offers you shelter without being paralyzed by fear of other's misunderstanding.

> God overcomes evil not by destroying it,
> but by outliving it.

In your Second Day, you may find your senses of touch, taste, and smell heightened. The food you once hurried past your tongue toward your stomach is now savored with a sigh. The cold wind is momentarily welcomed before you turn it away with scarf and gloves. The rain on the skin is another baptism. You find yourself sinking into the experience of the moment and, as you do, a tingling is felt in your hands as if electricity were scouting a path before shooting out from your fingers. These experiences were probably there in your First Day as well, but only in your Second Day do you know and name them.

When my soul is pure,
even the steam swirling above my teacup
is beautiful enough to light up my heart.

Second Day people often bristle against the nature of many relationships that are defined by context rather than Soul. Contextual friends exist within the container provided by work, role, neighborhood, religious community, or holidays. But when the job changes, the role dissolves, the new home is purchased across town, a new church becomes home, or the din of holiday gatherings recede, then the bowl breaks and the relationships flow out onto a thin surface and quickly evaporate. You are awakened to the disturbing realization that there is nothing deeper here than a relational accident involving a few bystanders with whom you have struck up a sequence of conversations strung end-to-end over a period of time. Contextual relationships feel conditional: I will be in relationship with you if you are nearby, convenient, or on my holiday party list.

Second Day people may find themselves loving and accepting others without the usual attachments and conditions society expects. You were brought out of the Night by an expansive and extraordinary love; how can you be alive and offer less? When you are companioned by the knowledge that every moment of your Second Day life is an unanticipated extension, you aspire to an open generosity, excited about the potential and wonder of each person you see. You desire to be a conduit of universal love. Those satisfied with a more confined understanding of relationships may find you enigmatic.

Confused family members tend to regard this sudden switch in behavior as oddly threatening, as if their loved one had become someone else. On the one hand, they may interpret the resistance of Second Day persons to participate in activities that are purely contextual (calendar driven gatherings, anonymous organizational functions, role-driven relationships) as indifference. Conversely they may feel uncomfortable with the depth of affection that Second Day persons may express for "no good reason." Yet, they may be intrigued and even a bit envious.

Whatever your beliefs or affiliation, you (as a Second Day person) have been granted the gift of a resurrection. In the Christian tradition, this experience has been patterned after Jesus who reemerged from his Night (crucifixion) into a Second Day (resurrection) and exhibited a transformed life. While Jesus experienced physical death on his journey toward a Second Day the Bible speaks of the new life we experience through God's love as a resurrection as well: "Since, then, you have been raised with Christ, set your hearts on the things above" (Colossians 3:1 NIV). A religious community may have been the conduit for the love that brought you back from the Night. A religious community may have been a factor in your descent into the Night. No matter. You have been the object of a divine intervention. You have been resurrected.

If you look to Christian scripture for guidance, it may be important for you to understand the difference between resuscitation and resurrection. Resuscitation is simply bringing a dead body back to life, brain, body, bone, and all. A resuscitated person gets up, goes home, and turns on a favorite television program. Nothing has changed. In contrast, resurrection is a transformation from one state of being to another. In resuscitation, you simply go back to life as you have always lived it. In resurrection, there is no going back.

A Second Day is not a First Day lived a second time. In the Christian tradition, the resurrected Jesus was a changed man. He did not return to the life he had lived. There was no haunting of the people who would not or could not accept him for who he was, no gliding up to Pontius Pilate to puff a "Boo!" in his face. Jesus spent time only with friends sharing his experience, his strength, and his hope. There was nothing contextual about this man's love. When he left town, indeed by some accounts even left this planet, he broke the bowl of time and space when he said, "In my heart I will always be with you. Don't forget me." Or literally: "And surely I am with you always, to the very end of the age" (Matthew 28:20 NIV). "Do this in remembrance of me" (1 Corinthians 11:24 NIV). These are the kinds of things that friends of the soul say to one another.

There are hearty lessons here. As a Second Day person you cannot return to your First Day. Even if you could, it would not be safe for you. In my First Day I habitually placed myself in situations where I would likely be rejected. It was a feeling to which I had become accustomed, a puzzle I was always trying to solve. Even now, in my Second Day, I am sometimes tempted to return to the scenes of my demise with the hope that this time I can solve the puzzle of my rejection and prevent it. For First Day people who find this difficult to understand, you might relate to the experience of watching a familiar movie and hoping it will turn out differently for your beloved character. Of course, it never does.

If you, like Jesus, are a Second Day person, spend as much time as possible in the nourishment of your soul. Find your Soul friends, those with whom you can exchange the mantra "In my heart, I will always be with you. Don't forget me." To find them, be a good Soul friend yourself and see what the universe sends your way. Some in your life will want you to come to your senses and return to the First Day. They may want you to justify your refusal. Neither apologize nor justify when faced with others' expectations. Arguments did not bring you out of the Night. You have been saved by the Love and Wisdom of the universe.

Rejoice for those in the First Day and do not wish for them to fully understand you. To fully understand would require that they pass through the Night, a trauma and a risk you dare not wish on others. It is important for Second Day people to cherish the life journey they have been privileged to walk.

If you are Second Day person, focus on sharing your experience, your strength, and your hope. Your experience will be helpful to those who have also walked this path and feel alone with their story. It will also provide understanding for survivors who have been savaged by the Night when it fell upon someone they loved.

> My enemies swung their swords, but what they cut was not me but the cords that bound me.

Share the strength you discovered on the way. Where did you find food for the journey? What cups of cold water kept you alive in the desert? Name names. Paint the faces. What fearful voice did you have to mute? What risk of love did you have to take? What emptiness did you have to allow to make room for what you needed most? Tell the story. Make it real.

And finally, share your hope. If Second Day people have nothing else to share, it is this—there is always hope. No defeat need ever be final. Do not place a period where a comma belongs. Ever. Some are in the Night, the darkest part. You may help them through the next minute and the next minute may be decisive. Sometimes, all we have to do is win one minute.

You don't have to be a Second Day person to make a life and death difference in someone's life. But you must follow your intuition. The story about Gwen at the beginning the book is a good example of how an expression of care, however awkward, can instill hope. Hope sometimes makes its flight on fragile wings and the strength that saves the voyage is momentarily borrowed from another. One minute of hope can be decisive.

I don't remember the precise date, but at some point near the beginning of 2005, I decided that I was going to live. That sounds backward to most people who think of a doctor pronouncing that verdict upon a person rather than a person pronouncing it upon himself. I suppose it is like announcing to folks that your funeral has been cancelled. It should be great news, but who knows how to respond to it?

Our Father
Who art in the earth
Fascinating be your name.
Your lure be strong
Your will a song
In heaven as here on earth.
Taste through us our daily bread
And forgive our willing slavery
As we forgive our fellow slaves.
And lead us into some awakening catastrophe
But deliver us from complacency.
For thine is the burning bush
The human touch
The beauty that must be true.
In the now that is all that we have.
Amen

People are reasonably well-prepared to respond to a death resulting from a terminal illness. Watch for the obituary. Send flowers. Call on the family. Give condolences. Say prayers. Wish for just one more moment of health for the diseased, just one more healthy Christmas. But when the wish is granted and death is cancelled, especially when the suicidal person chooses to live, people don't know what to do. The awkwardness is reminiscent of Tom Sawyer's funeral:

> As the service proceeded, the clergyman drew such pictures of the graces, the winning ways, and the rare promise of the lost lads that every soul there, thinking he recognized these pictures, felt a pang in remembering that he had persistently blinded himself to them always before, and had as persistently seen only faults and flaws in the poor boys. The minister related many a touching incident in the lives of the departed, too, which illustrated their sweet, generous natures, and the people could easily see, now, how noble and beautiful those episodes were, and remembered with grief that at the time they occurred they had seemed rank rascalities, well deserving of the cowhide. The congregation became more and more moved, as the pathetic tale went on, till at last the whole company broke down and joined the weeping mourners in a chorus of anguished sobs, the preacher himself giving way to his feelings, and crying in the pulpit.
>
> There was a rustle in the gallery, which nobody noticed; a moment later the church door creaked; the minister raised his streaming eyes above his handkerchief, and stood transfixed!
>
> First one and then another pair of eyes followed the minister's, and then almost with one impulse the congregation rose and stared while the three dead boys came marching up the aisle, Tom in the lead, Joe next, and

Huck, a ruin of drooping rags, sneaking sheepishly in the rear! They had been hid in the unused gallery listening to their own funeral sermon!

As Mark Twain's threesome discovered, not everyone may be congratulatory that you found a way to stay alive!

I have been helped by the insights of Othersiders who, upon recovering from some addiction, expected joyful celebrations from friends and family members and were disappointed when the response was tepid, barely causing them to look up from a rerun of "Do You Want to Be a Millionaire?"

"After all," Othersiders say, "it is normal for most people to be sober. You shouldn't expect to be congratulated for it!"

I suppose this is a helpful way to keep expectations low and ease disappointment. Still, I wonder about a society where we seem more celebratory over the victory of our favorite football team than we are when a brother or sister has slipped the grasp of suicide. I am reminded of the words of Jesus of Nazareth: "But we had to celebrate and be glad, because this brother of yours was dead and is alive again" (Luke 15:32 NIV).

In your Second Day, every day is a bonus.

ELEVEN

A Free Pass

I n the movie *Adaptation*, John Laroche (Chris Cooper) is a brilliant but gritty character in passionate pursuit of rare, exotic orchids. Passion is the thread of his life's narrative. He engages an obsession to the point of mastery only to suddenly drop it and move on to the next. In contrast to Laroche, Susan Orlean (Meryl Streep) is a journalist willingly trapped in a successful though pedestrian life. She is beguiled by the throb of vitality in Laroche's life story. After she listens to him describe the car accident that killed his wife and knocked out his two front teeth, she responds by saying that she envies people who have had a brush with death. "It's like a free pass," she says dreamily. "It gives you an excuse to change your life in any way you want. No one would blame you."

God is a clue leading to a clue leading to a clue.

It seems an odd way to respond to a person who has experienced such a tragedy, but it makes sense for persons like her. Susan Orlean is what I call a Ghosted Onesider. She has always lived on the same side of her life, the one that is always reasonable and, therefore, always stale. She has never experienced the excruciating pain and exhilarating joy of having to make a major change; everything is calculated to optimize her success. However, she haunts life like a ghost haunts a castle, trapped by a familiar space but only able to float through it without touching or being touched. Like a castle, the opportunities to escape through one drafty crack or another are many, yet she remains.

Ghosted Onesiders look with longing on Othersiders like John Laroche who have found it possible to flow from one side of life to another. But these stuck souls need an external event or agent that will justify the change. The life or death of their own Soul is never reason enough, unless, of course, it leads to thoughts of killing themselves.

This then is one of the spiritual functions of suicidal thinking: It provides the owner of the thought permission for change that he or she cannot seem to find any other way. It is the kind of "free pass" that Susan Orlean longs for. Much like drug addiction, suicidal thinking is obviously not the preferred path of change, but some of us just can't get to the best side of life without it.

When you realize that you are likely to kill yourself if you don't change your life (or at least live the rest of your life fighting that impulse), all reasons for inertia find their proper perspective. Second Day people have learned to identify and weigh the proper alternatives. The choice is no longer staying with a toxic career versus leaving a toxic career. It is leaving a toxic career versus dying. It is making the break with a religious organization versus dying. It is deciding that you will stop trying to keep everyone happy versus dying. You see the pattern here. As Mark Twain put it, death "has a wonderful effect of clarifying the mind."

I would rather have a God who is intelligent, than one who knows everything.

This is the potential gift that any pattern of self-destructive thinking brings to the Soul. Once you gain this insight, you give yourself permission to make the changes that you would never allow yourself to make otherwise. For those of us who thrive on permission, the threat of suicide gives the Soul an authority that we otherwise might never have allowed.

The threat of suicide gives Second Day persons permission to tend to their Souls. Taking the time to connect to the deepest part of your being and the universe of which you are a part is not a luxury. Neither is it a duty imposed by the expectations of others. It is the air we breathe. When the demands of others press in on this time, we have permission to say "No" because we are ultimately dealing with life and death not a simple time management issue.

The threat of suicide gives Second Day persons permission to choose the people with whom they spend their time and to limit their contact with those who are toxic or indifferent. Some people are not safe for Second Day persons to be around. Unfortunately, this may, and often does, include family members. The Soul of a Second Day person has the authority to decline invitations to family "celebrations" that leave them weakened, damaged, or at risk.

> Every man needs his own scripture,
> the record of his own personal revelation,
> the heavenly vision he must obey.

The threat of suicide also gives Second Day persons permission not to admit certain voices into their heads. Generally, I spend time weighing the merits of feedback given to me so that I can grow. Some voices, however, are arrows to the heart. They cannot be reasoned with or accommodated. They must be denied admission. Second Day persons may have had trouble doing this in their First Day since they might have felt guilty for refusing to listen. But when death is on the line, it is easier to place toxic voices on the other side of a soundproof shield and let them rant in silence.

Second Day people often naively hope that this shift in perspective will be equally convincing to the First Day people in their lives. Given the choice "you can either have me … divorced, single, gay, religious, non-religious, in AA, living with someone, fill-in-the-blank … or dead," First Day people often balk at the choice. That's because they tend to see suicidal thinking as an evil visitation upon an otherwise likeable soul.

First Day people often want a kind of exorcism. They want you to keep everything in your life the same, with the suicidal thinking cleanly removed. They believe that suicidal thinking is some evil that has snuck into your otherwise wonderful life; in fact, it is a symptom that your life needs to change, often radically. When the tire drops off the edge of the highway onto a rumble strip, the noise is not a sign that your tires should be removed; it is a signal that you need to turn the steering wheel in a different direction.

Freedom is only one side of the coin; it is always twinned with additional responsibilities. The most beautiful jewels always need a setting to hold, protect, and display them. Second Day persons might consider the gift they have been given as a jewel in need of a setting. How do they hold, protect, and display this Second Day?

For me this involves three things.

First, there is the "Never Even Once" list. This is the list of things I cannot afford to do even once. I am sure this list varies from person to person and will need to be discovered and developed on an individual basis. Here is my Never Even Once List.

1. I cannot isolate myself from my Othersouls when I am in great pain. Not even once.

2. I cannot seriously entertain any thought of killing myself without telling an Othersoul. Not even once.

3. I cannot put myself in situations where I am alone with firearms. Not even once.

Second there is the "Air Supply" list. I have done a little scuba diving in my life and I find it to be a combination of exhilaration and managed risk. This makes it a great analogy for me as a Second Day person because I know if I am going to experience a full and vibrant life, I must manage the risks involved. This means making sure I have adequate air for my life and soul. I cannot assign this responsibility to someone else. Every diver is responsible for his own gear. Here is my Air Supply list.

1. I will nourish the relationships of those to whom I have a solemn bond, particularly my wife, my children, and my mother. (My father died in 2003.) My love will always be an offering that they can accept or refuse without punishment or rejection.

2. I will invest in friendship. I will take the time and the initiative to discover and sustain relationships that exhibit mutuality, intimacy, loyalty, and gratitude.

3. I will insure that I have Othersouls in my life that know my history, understand my risks, and are prepared to receive my call if I am ever thinking about killing myself.

4. I will sustain an awareness that I am enfolded in a palpable field of goodness and love that guides and supports me. Included in this field are some people I call my Five Guys: my father, my uncle Don Waddell, my high school friend David Maze who was killed in Viet Nam, and two other friends, Paul Mendez and Ray Ferguson.

5. I will nurture my life with God through involvement with a spiritual community where available, but always with study, meditation, journaling, and engagement with the natural world.

6. I will be a good steward of my financial resources to avoid the kind of debt that leaves me feeling trapped and despairing.

Finally, there is my "Show and Tell" list. Having survived the Night of suicidal thinking, I feel a responsibility to reach out to others who are struggling with this lonely secret. I can never be whole if I simply leave others to the ravages of the darkness. But I am not simply a disinterested, detached conveyor of information. I have to step out of the black-hole with my story in hand. Right now there is only one item on my Show and Tell list.

1. Finish this book.

— TWELVE —

Caring for Your Soul

o one gives a damn about how you feel. They care about what you do." I suppose these words, spoken by a father to his coming-of age son, sum up adulthood as well as any. History judges men and women by the consequences of their actions and whether those actions advance or hinder the interests of the community. Communities—families, friends, employers, customers—have a right to expect responsible behavior that serves the common good.

There is a necessary corollary to this expectation. Except for a few rare individuals, no one is going to care for your Soul, the vitality and color of your being, the internal compass pointing you inexorably toward what you must do or what you must become. Few are going to encourage you to take up painting, write poetry, or leave a job that pays great money but is making it difficult for you to haul yourself out of bed in the morning. You will wait in vain for voices that ponder with you the purpose of your particular Soul, that rattle the bars of the mental prisons to which you may have sentenced yourself, or that speak the truth about your life that you are afraid to say out loud. And no one (with rare exception) will likely notice that you are running out of some ineffable, spiritual fuel unless it begins to impact your performance—in other words, what you do. This is the big boy, big girl reality of being an adult.

Some of us were thrust into the Night of suicidal thinking because we expected someone to care for our Souls who would not or, more likely, could not. This is not to say we did not have persons in our lives who loved us. Our personal relationships generally include persons who love us but who also depend on us to respond to life in a consistent pattern. Their well-being is linked to our consistency. However there are times when consistency is a death sentence.

"A rut is a grave with the ends kicked out," the saying goes. In those seasons of life when the gray routine of life is killing us, we need persons who can care for those parts of our lives that are unrecognized, unacknowledged, diminished, or even rejected. We need someone to care for our Souls. It is precisely here that we discover a painful truth. It is the flip side of the good Samaritan story: The persons who might have cared for our Souls didn't. Or couldn't.

During the years I served as an ordained minister I consulted with vocational counselors no less than six different times trying in desperation to find a way out. One of the six was a colleague who also was an ordained minister. He sat down with my wife and me, reviewed the situation, and summed it up this way: "You have a wife and four children. You are the sole means of support. That's a lot of responsibility. The only other field you are trained in is engineering. That has a short shelf life and is no longer of any value. Professional ministry is something you do well and is likely to have the greatest income potential of all your options. I think you need to stay in the ministry."

God and I would like to welcome you
to the Second Day of your life and
make our reservations for your future.

"But I am dying on the inside! Can't you see that I am dying?" I didn't say that, of course. I nodded and smiled my way out of his office. I could not argue with the reasonableness of his counsel. I probably would have said the same. What was I hoping for? I wanted someone to say what a woman named Azaria Akashi said several years later, "You look at life, and you see it differently. It is like looking at a color. You see green when others see blue. You cannot afford to be in a situation where you feel forced to deny your own reality. It is like a prison for you. Now that you are free, it is important that you be cautious about connecting with any organization that denies you the capacity to express your soul." That's what I needed to hear. It was years coming. And it would take me years to believe it.

It is difficult to accept the fact that you have invested so much of your life in something that is killing you. The disappointment of this discovery creates an open wound that feels too painful to bear. You keep returning to the source of your disappointment hoping that it will heal you, only to be wounded again. It may be a job, an abusive spouse, a chemical dependency, gambling, or pornography. For every person it is different. But your particular medicine of choice leaves you sicker.

> God is more like the earth than the sky.
> Even when we fall, we fall toward him.

There is an event from my childhood that provides an appropriate metaphor. I was probably five years old and living at that misty five-year-old level of awareness of what was actually happening in the dynamic of my family. We lived in one side of a two-story duplex on the west side of Columbus with a stairway running out of the dining room to the second floor. It seems to me that two-story floor plans must raise the volume of the average conversation in a family as people try to avoid the effort required to go up or down the stairs and instead yell from the top or bottom.

I don't recall most of the details of what happened. I remember my father standing at the top of the stairs and yelling for my mother to get the castor oil. I am not sure what particular malady calls for castor oil. I have never taken it, but the archived impression of its taste falls between worm slime and dog urine. Without knowing the particulars, I assumed my father was definitely not feeling well to resort to such a remedy.

My dad sent me from the top of the stairs to get the bottle of clear liquid that my mother was holding at the bottom of the stairs ("go-for" being one of the purposes of small children in two-story homes). I grabbed it out of my mother's hand and ran it up to my father who in one sweeping motion took it from my hand, removed the cap, and took a big swig of it straight from the bottle. I remember asking him if he should read the label first. Of course not. That was only for children learning in kindergarten how not to be poisoned.

It is further testimony to the special awfulness of castor oil that my father did not immediately recognize that he had actually downed several tablespoons of 6-12 insect repellant. He did pause with a reflective tilt to his head as if it took time for his body to register the chemical contradiction that had just hit his stomach. Now the label on the bottle seemed worth reading. With the dawning of comprehension, he simply cried out, "I just drank poison!"

You can imagine the many opportunities for blame and anger in the ensuing moments as panicked preparations were made to have my father's stomach pumped. The yelling up and down the stairs. The easily-confused bottles. The failure to read the label on both ends of the exchange. But beyond the multiple morals to the story is the simple reality that mistaking poison for medicine is a good way to ruin a sunny afternoon.

The problem with being soul-sick is that you keep turning to the same remedies that actually end up being poisons and only make you sicker. And in many cases there are no labels on the bottles to warn you. For me, I kept thinking that the church would become a community of healing for soul-sick folks. I wasn't consciously trying to construct that for myself. All I wanted was the healing that spilled from the glass of other people's overflowing lives, the crumbs from the table, using a biblical image. What I discovered was that the church, as an institution, has a life of its own. It will consistently move to protect itself, sometimes at the expense of the Souls of its members. Soul healing, in my experience, is not a realistic expectation for any institution; it is the domain of the personal and the individual.

Liberation
Every morning of a thousand days,
you put your paw to the gate.
But on one otherwise unremarkable day,
the gate yielded to this routine testing of your captivity.
In one fluid motion, you were loose upon the world,
terrified and terrifying.
You learned to hunt your food,
to sleep in the rain,
to stare down the grizzly
while bleeding from his puncture.
And now you know something that
for a time
will roll around in the marrow of your bones like an inner thunder.
Finally, one dark night when the moon rises full upon
the breeze it will become a thought:
I can never go back to the cage.

When people think about risks to the Soul, what generally comes to mind are things that are destructive to life's basic structure such as alcohol, drugs, criminal behavior, or destructive sexual behavior. True enough. Traditionally these are referred to as the sins of commission. What people often do not consider are the risks to the Soul that accrue to passivity and fear of change. These are sins of omission, more subtle, but no less deadly. The familiar can seem so innocuous, so safe. But if it is supporting a sickness of the Soul, it is as deadly as any chemical.

The Bible tells about a man who ran into a house to escape a bear. He slams the door shut behind him and breathes a sigh of relief. Exhausted from his narrow escape, he leans against a wall for support, only to be fatally bitten by a poisonous snake hiding in a hole in the wall. The house he thought was his rescue actually held his demise. In the Night, many of us came to realize that the major changes required for us to stay alive were not well received by some of those closest to us as "the uncles mutter, the women walk away, the young brother begins to sharpen his knife" (from "Maybe" by Mary Oliver).

The naïve child in us doesn't want to accept this realty. The child in us keeps waiting for someone to offer permission. The child in us keeps running back to one parental figure or another hoping someone will tend to our Souls. We begin to become adults only after we realize that we are responsible for our own Souls.

Second Day persons have often discovered this truth. Having postponed their own healing by an interminable waiting for permission, they have been given a gift by the Night. Their brush with death has been transformed into an encounter with the Light. In their darkest hour, they have followed the direction offered by this Light: "Tend to your Soul and you can live. But your quest for permission from others ends here."

Second Day persons realize that they are responsible for their own Souls. There is no one else to wait for and no one else to blame. Mistakes are theirs, but so are the lessons. Instead of citing the experiences of others, they cite their own. Instead of trying to mold their experiences to fit the experiences of others, they accept the plurality of the universe that God has made with its infinite capacity for variety.

> The closer we come to God's light,
> the wider we open our eyes.

Many people saw my leaving the ministry as a great victory for Satan. The acceptance of this line of thinking is what kept me stuck for years and brought me to the brink of death. In reality, my life outside the church is liberating. It enables me to serve God's world in rich and life-giving ways. I had breakfast this week with a man I had not seen since I was in the ministry. Somewhere near the middle of our time together he began, as others have, to place before me the view that I had been taken out of the ministry by Satan. In that conversation, I felt the familiar impulse to explain myself, to get his understanding and blessing (permission) for the work I am doing now. But then I remembered the gift of the Night: "Tend to your soul and you can live. But your quest for permission from others ends here."

I smiled in response. I said to him, "There are many different layers to our life experience, aren't there?" I felt a great love for him and a great appreciation for his place in my life.

I finished my day, picked up my wonderful wife (one of those rare persons who does care for my Soul), and we made tacos for supper. Sometime around the browning of the hamburger, I realized that I had walked away peacefully from eating breakfast with my friend without any thoughts of wanting to destroy myself. I had cared for him. I had cared for my own soul.

That's how I know I am in my Second Day.

THIRTEEN

A Second Day Spirituality

hen First Day persons consider the issue of suicide from a spiritual standpoint, their thoughts often go to the scriptures. For most, the matter is without cloud or confusion. The sixth commandment, "thou shall not kill," readily comes to mind. The word *kill* found in the commandment means more precisely "murder" and murdering anyone, including one's self, is a clear violation of God's sacred law. This appears decisive. First Day people often feel that no further exploration is necessary, and they stop at the certainty provided by threat of spiritual law. More painfully, those who have lost friends or family members to the Night of suicide may read these words with despair. Both redemption and mercy require us to take a deeper look.

Does the sixth commandment address the issue of suicide? The commandment might seem applicable did it not sit squarely within a larger set of commandments that clearly have the protection of others in mind, not oneself. If we are going to argue that the command not to kill includes not killing oneself, consistency would require us to say that the commandment not to steal also includes not stealing from oneself; the commandment not to covet includes not coveting the possessions of oneself; and the commandment not to commit adultery includes not "adultering" oneself. While psychology could make meaning of this with its modern and more compact understanding of the self, it is difficult to believe that the Hebrews had this in mind. There are repeated condemnations of murder found throughout the Bible, but they always have the protection of another person in the crosshairs, never oneself.

Love is the lamp of the soul.
Deny it at the wick and the whole house goes dark.

It may be surprising for some to realize that the word *suicide* never occurs in the Bible, and suicide as a topic is never addressed in any general way. Jesus does not mention it; neither does Paul. Since there are no general discussions of suicide, all our thinking about the subject must be developed around specific incidences of suicide found in the Bible and the biblical reactions to them. Most persons are surprised by the number of suicides in the Bible, not to mention the amount of suicidal thinking.

There are, of course, characters of negative standing in scripture who end their lives by suicide. However these persons were clearly diminished, not by their suicides, but by character flaws exhibited while living. King Saul suicides by falling on his own sword, but the sin that is most remembered is his visit to the witch of Endor in a proscribed search for guidance from a source other than God.

The Philistines find the dead king's body, cut off his head, and fasten the headless corpse to a wall. When the people of his hometown hear about it, they are not overcome with shame that their favorite son has suicided. On the contrary, they send their bravest soldiers on a dangerous mission to retrieve the body. After burial, they fast for seven days. Contrast this with many western religious bodies that have historically refused to allow religious services or burial for those who die by suicide.

All Sunday school children know of Judas, who either hanged himself or fell headlong in a field and burst open depending upon which obituary one favors. But again, Judas is remembered for his act of betrayal, recalled in every celebration of the Eucharist. The words are not "on the night in which Judas suicided" but "on the night in which Jesus was betrayed." The focus is on the injury Judas inflicted on another, not himself, and on how he lived his life not how he ended it.

> We think we are brilliant because we have discovered the laws of the universe.
> It never occurs to us that the part of the universe that runs on laws may be a cork floating on a vast ocean of pure freedom.

Not everyone who suicides in scripture is remembered negatively. Consider Samson. Samson, you may recall, is the Popeye of the Bible whose strength accrued to the length of his hair rather than a spinach-rich diet. While held in custody by the Philistines, a blinded Samson knowingly brings down the roof by pushing out a load-bearing wall. He kills himself and takes a number of civilian men and women with him. His suicide is not seen as an evil deed but as the final heroic act indicative of his best self, a warrior leader. In his self-inflicted death, Samson demonstrates three surface reasons that people consider suicide: to punish, to control, or to escape an unpleasant future.

For one man in scripture, suicide is portrayed as the carefully reasoned decision of a bright and insightful mind. Ahithophel is described as one whose advice was "like that of one who inquires of God." He begins as advisor to King David, but a number of years after David's fiasco with the married Bathsheba and his murder of her husband, Ahithophel throws in his lot with Absalom, David's son. Absalom has instigated a successful civil war against his father and turns to Ahithophel for advice on how to manage the end game. Ahithophel advises quick pursuit by a relatively small, but agile force of twelve thousand men. Absalom rejects the good advice of Ahithophel and delays until he can assemble a larger force.

Ahithophel is smart enough to foresee the outcome of Absalom's error and what it spells for his own future. Well before the rebellion is crushed and Absalom is killed, Ahithophel saddles his donkey and rides home. There he promptly puts his affairs in order and then hangs himself. There is no condemnation of Ahithophel in the text. Indeed he is buried in his father's tomb. Once again, contrast this act of compassion with the church of the Middle Ages that refused burial in holy ground to those who died by suicide and even "tortured their bodies" by hanging them, beheading them, or dragging their corpses through the streets.

The Bible also describes characters who suicide by enticing others to kill them. This is called "suicide by proxy." A depressed Jonah flees the call of God by sea only to find the ship he has boarded threatened by a great storm. Jonah convinces the crew that if they will throw him overboard, the storm will cease and they will be saved. As we know, a great fish intervenes but this is only a temporary fix for Jonah. His suicidal thinking reemerges at the end of the story when reality fails his expectations. "He wanted to die, and said, 'It would be better for me to die than to live'" (Jonah 4:8 NIV). Jonah's actions are never described as suicidal behavior, and his wish to die is never described as suicidal thinking. But that's what it is.

Stop trying to ascend to heaven with a placid smile and lit face.
You'll only arrive to discover that God is not there.
God has descended into the earth. Fall into your body.
There is more of God in your dancing than in your fasting.

Here we see the tricky nature of deciding what constitutes suicide and what does not. Think of how this story would strike someone in the Night of suicidal thinking. If it is legitimate for Jonah to arrange for his own death as a way of saving his fellow passengers from a raging sea, is it less legitimate for a man in desperate economic straights to provide a life-saving insurance payout to his family through his own death?

Indeed, think about how the intentional death of Jesus might strike someone who believes that people will be better off if he or she dies. According to the record, Jesus is virtually certain that his entry into Jerusalem will provoke the authorities to kill him. His followers are sure of this as well. The only question in their minds is whether they should go and die with him. Jesus does not have to go to Jerusalem and die. In the Catholic liturgy of the Eucharist, his death is referred to as one he freely chose. Jesus comes to peace with provoking his own murder through the belief that his death will ultimately be of benefit to others.

Some would argue that Jesus is a unique figure in this regard and his actions offer no guidance regarding our own life and death decisions. This approach sacrifices the shared humanity of Jesus and forces a rethinking of the popular question "What would Jesus do?"

Others might suggest that few people who suicide are actually thinking about their death benefitting others; they are merely trying to escape some external or internal pain. There is no question that this is true for many in the Night of suicidal thinking. But there are a sizable number of people who think "others would be better off without me" or "I don't want my family to have to go through this." This is not so far from the statement of Jesus: "It is for your own good that I am going away" (John 16:7 NIV). In fact when Jesus said, "Where I go, you cannot come" (John 8:21 NIV) the Jews interpreted his words as a reference to suicide: "Will he kill himself?" (John 8:22 NIV).

I am not suggesting that the Bible advocates suicide. I am pleading for folks to put themselves in the mindset of a person thinking of killing himself or herself. If you were to push a Bible beneath the eyes of a person in the Night of suicidal thinking and ask them to read it cover to cover, the stories summarized above are what they would encounter. What might they learn from such stories?

- Some biblical persons suicide because they have failed to such an extent that they feel themselves beyond redemption (Saul, Judas).

- Some suicide because they have carefully and rationally calculated that they are going to die at the hands of others and would rather die by their own hand (Ahithophel).

- Some suicide as a way of punishing other people who they believe are living in opposition to God (Sampson).

- Some suicide by proxy as a way of providing others a better future (Jonah's attempt).

- People in the Bible are generally evaluated by how they lived rather than how they died.

- For the most part, people in the Bible who die by suicide are remembered lovingly and with compassion by their family and community.

- Suicide is never offered as a desirable outcome to one's life.

For those of you in the Night of suicidal thinking, these stories might help you feel less alone at a time when isolation is life threatening. Even in the scripture, suicidal thinking is more common than might be supposed. It occurs in the lives of governing officials, politically savvy advisors, physically powerful warriors, and great revivalist preachers. Reading these stories might also generate anger if you contrast the compassion in the scripture (on the whole) with the absence of compassion that you actually experience in many religious communities.

First Day persons may be struck by the many different and conflicting thoughts and feelings in the same Bible. The diversity of experiences found within the scripture should save us from a rush to judgment regarding the topic of suicide. At the very least it should evoke compassion and mercy rather than condemnation.

karamay [k ä r- ä -m ä]
I miss you. I am not the same without you.

Both First Day and Second Day persons seek a spiritual path that will bring healing into the life of persons dwelling in the Night of suicidal thinking and hopefully prevent their deaths. Where is the "balm of Gilead?" Christian theology typically locates the death of Jesus as the locus of salvation. For those trying to make their way out of the Night and into a Second Day, the death of Jesus may not be the aspect of his life that is the most compelling. It is well-known in the suicide prevention community that an indiscriminant celebration of a person's life after a suicide invites a contagion of similar behavior among those who are already thinking about killing themselves. Focusing on the death of Jesus as a path to a better life beyond death has not proven protective for many people in the Night of suicidal thinking.

Many Second Day people have found it helpful to focus on a different point of the gospel narrative, namely, the entry of Jesus into the world. "The people walking in darkness have seen a great light" (Isaiah 9:2 NIV) is the promise of the prophet Isaiah, fulfilled in the Gospel of Luke. What is this light, romanced in story and symbolized by Epiphany's star? It is the revelation of a fundamental life-altering truth: The fullness of God's love cannot be expressed by words alone. To fully experience "God with us" requires a human, a flesh and blood person. This ideal was brought to life in Jesus of Nazareth who went about delivering people from every form of darkness. His ministry of "God with us" continues to be expressed by human beings who are now referred to as "his body."

There are three kinds of persons in my world:
Those who walk as fast as I do,
Those I slow down for,
Those who are with me at all speeds.

It is clear from the research that being a part of a spiritual community can be a protective factor for many who are thinking about killing themselves. It is equally clear that it is not the particular belief system that is protective. It is the presence of the community itself. Our creedal statements and doctrines have little power to save a person in the Night from falling into eternity. But our presence as a sacramental expression of the love of God can be decisive! When we understand that we are God's hands, every encounter is potentially lifesaving. When this attitude is carried in the soul of a community, hospitality is elevated from the status of "friendliness" to the "touch of life." We offer God's love as a holy wonder: "I wonder if my presence is saving your life today?" You never know.

I would argue that Christmas should be claimed by people of the Second Day. (The belief that December has the highest suicide rate is simply another in a long list of myths. That dubious distinction belongs to April.) What a wonderful time to give to one another the present of your presence by renewing this pledge: "As far as it is in our power, you will never be alone and you will never lose hope. Stay with us. We would not be the same without you." This simple renewal would rescue the holiday season from the trite commercialism that everyone knows is hollow. It would potentially save thousands of lives and millions of injuries. Can you think of a better Christmas?

The message of Christmas is not simply that God has come into the world through Jesus. It is that the love and goodness in the world is always an expression of a larger love at work on our behalf. Because of Christmas, we not only say, "Thank God for Jane!" but also "Thank Jane for God!" I would not know God apart from Jane . . . and Bob and Rick and Sue and . . . others. Christmas shows us that we know more about God from a human experience of love than we could ever know from words alone. Every person who loves us is our "Merry Christmas," no matter when in the course of a year we experience their acts of love.

> Some things are too beautiful not to be true.
> If something beautiful in the world turns out to be false,
> it is usually because the beauty we thought was in the
> world, was really inside us all along.

Most of us (Second Day people) were delivered from the darkness and saved from our own self-destruction by expressions of the love of God that came our way in flesh and blood human beings. In my Second Day, I can name each one of them. I celebrate their nativities. Jesus' birth in the world gives dignity and purpose to every other birth. Every birth expresses the potential of "God with us" in whatever stall that particular life happens to be "mangered."

When we know that God is with us (not against us) through the presence of a compassionate community, our chances of surviving the Night and entering a Second Day infinitely improve. Is there a biblical passage that illumines this reality? Fortunately there is:

> About midnight Paul and Silas were praying and singing hymns to God, and the other prisoners were listening to them. Suddenly there was such a violent earthquake that the foundations of the prison were shaken. At once all the prison doors flew open, and everybody's chains came loose. The jailer woke up, and when he saw the

prison doors open, he drew his sword and was about
to kill himself because he thought the prisoners had
escaped. But Paul shouted, "Don't harm yourself! We are
all here!" (Acts 16:25-29 NIV).

Here we see how God, working through a flesh-and-blood
community, averts the suicide of a Philippian jailor who
concluded too quickly that his life was over. What do we learn
from this incredible passage about how to engage a person in
the Night of suicidal thinking?

We must see the person at risk. Paul did. Was the jailor
standing in front of Paul in plain view? Did Paul surmise that the
man might be in trouble and seek him out? Both possibilities
are before us in the people we know. A few Night people are in
plain view. They let us know clearly and directly that they are
thinking about suicide. Unfortunately the number of people
who have the capacity to do this is relatively small. People who
are thinking about suicide are generally depressed. Their energy
level is low and it is difficult for them to broach a subject that
most people are uncomfortable talking about even though they
desperately want to.

This means that the community must bear the burden of
raising the subject. Sermons should address the issue of suicide
and suicidal thinking as a significant and common human
problem. Pastoral prayers should recognize that a significant
number of persons in a congregation are generally thinking
about suicide and need the gift of hope and love. In addition,
members should be equipped to become comfortable asking
people if they are thinking about suicide. They need help getting
past the myths about suicide, namely, that asking about suicide
would put it in someone's head.

Suicidal thinking is extremely common. On average, about
thirty persons in a congregation of five hundred are thinking
about their own suicide on any given Sunday. I try to make this
concrete with the following observation.

Suppose you were to hear that someone was thinking about killing thirty of your adult members and ten members of your youth group. You would pray, sound warnings, call police, take protective measures, and pray some more. But because the potential killer is the member himself or herself, nothing is done.

Given the prevalence of suicidal thinking in a typical congregation, and given the fact that it will be an issue over the life span of nearly everyone, it makes sense that it be addressed sacramentally. If we circumscribe marriage, ordination, confirmation, and baptism with vows, doesn't it make sense that we call members to take a vow that they will disclose suicidal thinking when it occurs in their lives especially since life and death are on the line? This is a vow that could be remembered and recalled at critical junctures—death of a spouse, retirement, divorce, loss of employment, entering high school, going off to college.

We must be clear about our role. "Do not harm yourself." Church members are not being called to become amateur therapists. We are seeking to stop suicidal behavior. It is unrealistic for members to think that they can stop a person from thinking about suicide. Suicidal thinking generally develops over a long period of time and requires a significant reworking of mental and emotional processes. Suicidal behavioral, on the other hand, can often be prevented through the call of a persistent and loving voice. This saving act is possible for anyone and appropriate to a body that lays claim to the priesthood of all believers.

We must claim the power of a present community. Over time, suicidal thinking wears down the inner resources of the Soul. When faith, hope, meaning, purpose, and confidence are depleted it takes time for their replenishment. Community, on the other hand, can be restored relatively quickly if people are willing to be present to the person at risk. This is the critical resource as Paul notes: "Do not harm yourself. We are all here."

Notice that a de facto church discipline of isolation works exactly counter to this Bible verse. It is an accepted fact that the risk of suicide increases dramatically when a person is socially isolated. Here the faith community must take a hard look at itself and its de facto practice of church discipline. While the formal discipline of church members is largely a thing of the past, a more informal process is often at work. Many churches no longer practice excommunication and those that do are loose in its formal application. However the enforcement of solitude upon impenitent souls has a significant history in spiritual communities. Penitentiaries were originally designed for just this purpose.

When certain members disappoint the community, the reaction is often one of forced solitude. This is expressed by outright exclusion, removal from group rosters, avoidance, passive response to absence, termination of contact, refusal to return phone calls, or moving down the ladder of meaningful communication (from face-to-face conversations to phone calls, from phone calls to letters, from letters to emails, from emails to silence). This de facto church discipline is extremely powerful. But it is also unarticulated and therefore unregulated. Because it is not named, it can easily be denied. This adds an element of "crazy making" to it. The person experiences the force of the isolation and at the same time is made to believe that the isolation isn't really happening. At the very moment that a community holds the potential to protect a life from injury or death, the community withdraws.

A contradiction in our souls is two drops that have not yet found their way to the one ocean.

Contrast this with the words of Paul: "Do not harm yourself. We are all here."

There is every indication that most suicides are preventable. However, prevention requires two things. People who are thinking about suicide must feel safe telling others, and people who suspect that someone else is thinking about suicide must feel comfortable asking them about it.

I can either trust your imperfect vision or my
imperfect vision.
If I trust yours then I will learn your lessons,
but I will be truant from the school of my own Soul.
I will spend my life unable to tell you my real name.

Because the obstacles to saving lives from suicide are primarily emotional and spiritual, the church is ideally positioned to address this issue. It does not require capital expansion, new sound systems, or changes in worship format. What it requires is conversion: a basic emotional/spiritual reorientation of the community. We must come to understand that the Night of suicidal thinking is not something rare or unexpected. Many of us will enter that Night in our years upon this planet. We must also help one another realize that our goal is not simply to keep people from dying in the Night. It is to help them find their Second Day and the joyful hope that this new day brings.

At its best, a ministry of suicide prevention is actually a ministry of life preservation. Resilience is the ability of a Soul to bounce back from adversity. Historically, Christians excel at resilience because forethought has been given to the resources needed to face adversity. Resources that contribute to resilience include strong relationships, sources of meaning and hope, joyful service to others, solid financial resources, vocational integrity, and so forth.

One source of theological reflection along these lines is the call to readiness found in the doctrine of the second coming of Christ (a theme of Advent). This is not merely a call to be ready to die. It is a call to be ready to face the adversity that accrues to moments of crisis. It is a call developed, not from a somber preoccupation with future tribulation, but from a wise investment in the things that sustain the abundant living that Jesus promised us: "I have that they may have life, and have it to the full" (John 10:10 NIV).

— FOURTEEN —

Will the Sick One Stand?

A woman comes into the coffee shop where I am writing this book. We strike up a conversation. She asks me what I am doing. I tell her I am writing a book about suicide. She tells me the story about her cousin who had suicided. "She was brilliant," she says several times. The cousin was a nurse who later attended medical school, one of two women who graduated in her class. Several years later her brother suicided. "Also brilliant," she says several times. "Gay. Came out of the closet, but then couldn't deal with it. Hanged himself."

I tell her how prevalent suicide is. Third-leading killer of high school students. Second-leading killer of young adults. Older adult males dying at five times that rate (deaths per 100,000 persons). She agrees that it must be more prevalent than most of us realize. She mentions a time in her life when the lights came on about the prevalence of suicide.

She tells me about a large gathering she had attended to hear a well-known speaker. At some point the speaker wished to locate a woman in the audience who had spoken to him prior to the start of the meeting. The particular woman had indicated to the speaker that her brother had hanged himself. I don't remember if she told me the topic of the speech or the nature of the audience,

111

but it must have made what happened next feel appropriate. The speaker asked for the person in the audience whose brother had killed himself to please put up a hand. It wasn't just one hand that went up. Several hands went up all over the audience!

"It was then that I realized how many people had been touched by suicide," she said.

First Day persons often say that those who are thinking about suicide are irrational. Gather around ye pots; the kettle speaks! We have been told by David Litts, the head of the Surgeon General's effort to prevent suicide, that people kill themselves for many reasons but it basically boils down to two: a loss of hope and a loss of social connection. For readers who are old enough, think back to 1960. At that time it was extremely risky for a man to tell his family and community that he was gay. What did the society of 1960 systematically withhold from a gay person? Opportunities for employment, housing, leadership, holding public office, and so forth. You might lump all those under the category of hope.

But that's not all that is withheld. Companionship. Friendship. Spiritual fellowship and more. You might lump all those under the category of social connection. Here is the irrational part. A society withholds hope and social connection from a person or a group of persons, then expresses shock when socially alienated persons kill themselves! This is irrational!

This is not a poem. It definitely is not,
for if it were
the last word would rhyme
With "not"
And it didn't.
It would be taught or tot or taut . . .
And it isn't.

Far from being irrational, people in the Night of suicidal thinking often have twenty-twenty vision on the reality of the society to which they are connected. They understand how harsh a community can be on people either because of their sexual orientation, their lifestyle, their weight, their appearance—or the fact that they just happen to be in a bully's bull's-eye and no one seems interested in doing anything about it. Or it could be that they are simply brilliant, and people with gifted minds are often isolated and punished for their non-conformity. Whatever the case, they understand that the community around them is withholding from them the two things they most desperately need: hope and social connection. They realize this is having a deadly effect on their lives. They accurately perceive the relationship between what people are doing and how it is affecting them.

What is divine in you will always be crucified by something or someone.

First Day people often will not face the reality of how they are treating someone in the Night and the likely impact of that treatment. Creating situations in our communities where individuals are deprived of hope and social connection, and then being shocked when these situations have detrimental, even deadly impacts is insanity. The sane approach would be to change how we interact with other people, especially those in the Night. As Einstein put it, "The definition of insanity is doing the same thing over and over while expecting a different result."

I was speaking with a First Day person several years ago after a suicide awareness training. She was a sweet woman who spoke with an anguished voice and lots of tears. She told me the story of her brother who had left his wife for another woman. As a Christian, she felt that she had to demonstrate her disapproval of his action; she did so by cutting off all contact with her brother. Now word was coming to her through other family members that her brother was thinking about suicide. She felt torn. On the one hand, she wanted to be true to her Christian convictions that his behavior was wrong. On the other hand, she was worried that her brother would suicide and that she would always feel guilty.

Now as compassionate as I felt for this dear soul, she was being as irrational as any person contemplating suicide. She wanted two things that are logically contradictory. She wanted to be able to discipline her brother by withholding her relationship, an act that increases his risk of suicide, while simultaneously being assured that she was not increasing his risk of suicide. She did not perceive that there might be other ways of expressing concern for her brother's behavior that would not be potentially lethal. She was unable to distinguish the critical difference between acceptance and endorsement.

The gift that Second Day people often have to offer is bringing the clarity of their thinking, albeit through pain, to First Day people who assume that they are behaving in perfectly rational ways.

A newspaper carried an interesting story of a village in Chiapas, Mexico. It seems that the cattle of the village became jittery and ran toward higher ground. The residents, most of whom were in bed, got up and began chasing after the jittery livestock with shotguns and rifles. When they reached the top of the hill where the cattle had taken refuge, they turned to watch a landslide suddenly destroy their village. Since most of the villagers were on top of the hill instead of snug in their beds, nearly all of them—600 persons—were spared. The "loco cattle" had felt something was wrong and had instinctively responded to it. But it took the community a while to realize what was happening. Here we have the classic reversal of spirituality that we have already noted. What first seems to be irrational to the community ends up making sense, while the supposedly rational behavior turns out to be flawed. The first is last; the last, first.

Suicidal thinking is not simply the irrational disturbance of a few "sick" people who need to be pitied by the "rational" majority. It is a signal that something is wrong in the entire system. We live in a world that is, in the words of Leonard Sweet, a suicide machine. We are moving inexorably toward living on a planet with CO_2 levels so high that it cannot support human life as we know it. Is this not irrational? We are rightly traumatized by the 3,000 deaths caused by the attack of 9/11. As an expression of our outrage, we attack a country that had no connection whatsoever to that tragedy. We are so energized by the 9/11 attack that we will spend close to $3,000,000,000,000 on that war. But we are largely inured to the fact that jets could crash into twin towers every month, month after month, and you still would not equal the number of people who die from suicide every year. Is this not irrational?

Every suicide is a tragedy with a face. There are also faces left behind as family members and friends gaze into the empty spaces and try to cope with the silence. Suicide quilts sewn together from the photographs of those lost in the darkness are giving suicide a human face.

Every suicide is also a hologram of our global community, an emblematic warning that something is seriously wrong, not just for the person who completed or attempted suicide, but for us all. When the canary stops singing its song, all songs are at risk. Suicide is for human beings what the melting of the global icecaps is for the environment: a sign that we are not paying enough attention to the health of the networks on which all our lives depend. The mechanism that has enabled us to live in denial of the impact of global warming is the same mechanism that keeps us from asking the hard question about suicide: "Why do so many people in our 'advanced' societies want to kill themselves?"

I do not believe this is simply one question among many. I believe it is the question of our day. If we find the courage to face the question of suicide and address it, many other questions will be answered in the process. A world where most people have enough hope and connection to want to live out their natural lives on this planet and learn the spiritual lessons assigned them, is a world that is healthy and welcoming for every creature that God has created.

— FIFTEEN —

Second Day Persons

Anyone who has toured the ancient ruins of Greece can hardly help but wonder how the Greeks constructed the massive stone columns holding up the porticos of those majestic buildings. I was no exception, but I pondered the question in silence waiting for an opportune moment to pose the question to our guide. I didn't have to. If you drive up to the parking lot near the top of Mount Athena and then hike the rest of the way to the Acropolis you find yourself standing in front of the Parthenon. Make your way around the right side of the building to the edge of the mountain and you will discover a long, rectangular pile of stones. These are the stones that the builders rejected.

Do one thing that scares you every day.

However, they did not reject them immediately. Having gone to all the trouble of hauling them up the mountain, they had performed the initial work required to make them fit. Most of the stones have been shaped to serve as one component or another in the building. Included in the pile are the aborted sections of columns, circular cylinders roughly four feet tall and three feet in

123

diameter. Lying unused in a pile, the secret of their construction is exposed. A square keyway had been cut in the center of each section. In the final construction the sections were stacked one on top of the other and rotated so that their keyways were aligned. Then the builders inserted a tight-fitting, square-shaped wooden post down through the center. This served to keep them vertically aligned and stable.

I was struck by this experience. Here was the lesson I took away. If you want to see a beautiful building, look at the Parthenon. If you want to learn how to construct a beautiful building look at the stones that the builders rejected.

If you are a Second Day person, I dare say that you have had strong encouragement to toss the dark season of your life into the pile of rejected experiences. It is not the part of your life that you want people to see, certainly not at first look, possibly not at all. Most of us want to appear competent, successful, and "together." Unfortunately, we don't learn much by gazing at competent, successful, and together people. We learn by going around to the side and observing the process by which the person was built.

The experiences we reject as useless or painful often turn out to be the ones that are decisive in our development. They hold the most important lessons for others and for ourselves. Those lessons are lost as long as we are black-holed by shame. When we step out and claim our Second Day experience we also make its lessons available to others.

Many people teeter on the line between life and death. Equally important is the fact that literally millions totter on the line between hope and despair, between love and isolation, between exuberant living and stifling boredom. The concern is not simply that these millions will attempt suicide—it is that they will never really attempt living either. They will live out their days beneath commercial loudspeakers of various types pounding out a message of their inadequacy and, for many, punctuated by their own thoughts of killing themselves. No one will help them understand the meaning of the suicidal impulse. They will learn well enough that their impulse is wrong. They will be shamed into silence. They will be scolded into compliance. Usually, no one will teach them that while their impulse is wrong, the wisdom of the Soul is basically right. They are spiritually gasping for air.

This task of spiritual development should presumably fall to existing spiritual communities: churches, synagogues, mosques. In reality, organized religions have largely failed the task of helping people develop vibrant, thriving Souls. Research is beginning to confirm what many have suspected all along—there is no connection between the level of engagement of members with their religious communities and their own spiritual vitality.

As people live longer, the need for personal reinvention will increase. If you are a leader of a spiritual community, an important opportunity lies before you—developing your church, synagogue, or mosque as a place that excels in its ability to help members reinvent their lives. This reinvention is not a one-time event addressed by a single conversion experience. The need of long tenured Christians to reinvent their lives should not be seen as a sign that the first conversion "didn't take." If spiritual communities will normalize reinvention of the self and develop resources to support persons during that process, it would not only protect individuals from desperation, it would contribute to a more vibrant community.

As a Second Day person, there are steps you can take that will be of help to others. Here are a few:

1. Reflect on your story. You may never have done this before in any intentional way. (The outline on page 129 may help you.)

2. Reflect on the lessons you have learned from your experience. (The outline on page 130 may help you.)

3. Get clear on how you are going to hold, protect, and share your Second Day. (The outline on page 130 may help you.)

4. Share your story. As you are ready, look for opportunities to break the silence of suicide. Stay focused on your primary objective: caring for others who are struggling. Don't let the focus get shifted to you.

5. Get trained. If you begin to share your story, people will come to you for help and support. Training will give you a "smart ear" so that you will know how to listen and what to do.

6. Pay attention to your gut. If you get a flash thought that someone is in trouble or pain, ask him or her. Call and reach out in any way you feel you can. Send a card or leave a voice mail. Anything. Remember, people in the Night are in unbelievable, unbearable pain. They may not be able to reach out to you for help. They need you to reach out to them.

7. Make connections. As you share your story, invite other Second Day people to identify themselves to you. Share your experience, your strength, and your hope.

I finish this chapter on Good Friday, 2008. According to Christian tradition, on this day the best elements of society—its most prestigious religious, economic, and political leaders—put to death the man who most clearly represented God's intention for a human Soul, Jesus of Nazareth. You do not have to be a person who accepts Christian doctrine to appreciate the message. Society has a tendency to attack the source of its own individual and community health. Good Friday represents a kind of corporate suicide attempt. A community crucifies the Divine living in its midst and thereby drives a dagger into its own heart. The entire land falls into the Night. In the biblical account, darkness engulfs the region for three hours beginning at noon. What should have been the brightest moment of the day, high noon, becomes its darkest.

Good Friday reveals that the darkness of the suicidal impulse is not rare or peripheral to the human condition. The attack that brings such darkness to our Souls is not carried out by the worst of our society but by the very aspects of living we consider to be fundamental to a normal life: marketing, media, ubiquitous messaging, and a frantic pace of life that allows little space for tending our inner lives. Good Friday has the power to save our Souls, not by providing a sacrifice to satisfy God's need for vengeance, but by revealing our need to consciously and courageously resist the forces of the Night that are indifferent or even hostile to what is necessary for healthy Souls to flourish in our communities and in our individual beings.

> Every man must hold his own against
> the voices of the universe,
> not just the evil ones,
> but the inspired, beautiful ones as well.
> He must not turn his voice over to any other,
> however beautiful, inspiring, or insightful it be.
>
> Against the artist, he must bring his own art.
> Against, the poet, his own poetry.
> Against the orator, his own speech.
>
> Ironically, if a man can only recite the words
> of another he has sold his Soul to the devil,
>
> because he has banished his own voice
> to the outer darkness.

In two days, it will be Easter, the Second Day after the crucifixion. The Second Day is a day of resurrection. Deep within the mystery of our hearts, there is part of us that is unwounded and untrammeled, waiting to burst forth into an exuberant and vital life. Botanists discovered long ago that there are seeds that will not germinate in the spring unless first they have been frozen in the depth of a winter night. Some of us will enter our Second Day only by passing through the darkest of Nights.

Second Day persons have an opportunity to engage in one of life's most rewarding endeavors—helping people discover a life truly worth living. By offering the gifts of hope and friendship with a commitment to the dignity and beauty of the Soul, we discover a simple, yet profound mission:

In the next ten minutes, someone will choose to live.

If you are considering suicide please call

1-800-SUICIDE

Your Second Day Experience

Your Story

What was your attitude toward suicide during your First Day?

What experiences shaped your First Day thinking about suicide?

How and when did your First Day come to an end?

How did suicide first become an option for solving a problem?

What was your experience of the Night?

What helped keep you alive?

Who were the Othersouls that helped you through the Night?

When and how did your Second Day begin to dawn?

Your Lessons

What have you learned that would be valuable for:

☀ First Day people who have never seriously considered suicide but are concerned for people that they love?

☀ People in the Night who are struggling with suicidal thinking?

☀ People in their Second Day who have learned how to live in a way that does not require that they think about how to kill themselves?

What important lessons have you learned through this experience that are important for everyone?

What is your message to the communities of which you are a part (workplace, spiritual, friendships, family)?

How You Hold, Protect, and Share Your Second Day

What is on your "Not Even Once" list? (Things you cannot afford to do, even once.)

What is on your "Air Supply" list? (Things you must do to insure that you have adequate air for your life and soul.)

What is on your "Show and Tell" list? (Things you must do to reach out to others who are struggling with this lonely secret.)

About the Author

J Russell Crabtree earned a degree in engineering physics from The Ohio State University in 1972. He worked for three years in research and development at the Eastman Kodak Company before earning a Masters of Divinity degree from Fuller Seminary. He served as a Presbyterian minister until 1998 when he left pastoral ministry and began working full-time to develop a home for children with HIV in Honduras, Montana de Luz. His experience in Honduras, combined with his own spiritual development, led to such a period of transformation that he adopted his pen name on May 5, 2005 (05-05-05): Fe Anam Avis.

In the aftermath of three suicides in his community, he and Linda Karlovec, PhD, founded The Community Response Team, a cross-professional coalition representing parents, schools, churches, medical professionals, and mental health experts. He was recruited by Melinda Moore to serve as the chief operating officer of the newly formed Ohio Coalition for Suicide Prevention, which wrote the suicide prevention plan for the state of Ohio and created cross-professional suicide prevention coalitions at the county level.

He received suicide intervention and awareness training in 2002. Soon afterward, he founded a company called BestMinds, LLC, aimed at "helping persons find their best minds in times of personal crisis." He began working with county coalitions in southeast Ohio, developing suicide prevention plans and conducting awareness training. Since beginning that work, he has trained thousands of people across the state of Ohio and in West Virginia.

In 2003, he worked with Dr. David Litts who was heading the Surgeon General's effort at suicide prevention in the United States and developing guidelines for clergy conducting memorial and funeral services for those who had died by suicide.

In 2003, he also became engaged in the issue of domestic violence. He was asked to write an intervention training curriculum by the Columbus Coalition Against Family Violence to be used in faith communities. Using that curriculum, Breaking the Silence, he has trained hundreds of people in scores of churches to deal with family violence.

He has written a number of books and articles including *The Elephant in the Boardroom*; *Mountain of Light*; *The Fly in the Ointment: Why Denominations Aren't Helping Their Congregations and How They Can*; and *Owl Sight: Evidence-Based Discernment and the Promise of Organizational Intelligence for Ministry*.

Fe Anam Avis lives in Greenville, South Carolina, with his wife Shawn. He has four children, Emily, Elizabeth, Sarah, and Michael. Contact information can be found on his website at www.aseconddayy.com.